Advance Praise for *Cl...*
Ten Proven Strategies to Transform Your Life

"Diane Altomare presents a powerful, experiential, and practical path for using obstacles and issues of the past to mobilize us through the gateway of liberation. Let Altomare guide you, with stories and exercises, on this most important journey back to yourself. It's the only one that will ever matter!"

—**NANCY LEVIN**
Best-selling author of *Jump . . . And Your Life Will Appear*

"I've been fortunate enough to work with Diane Altomare. Through her coaching I've been able to tap into my own strength to navigate through both good and tough times. Reading *Clarity*, I can so vividly hear her voice and I am so excited that now countless others can draw on her special expertise to become who they are meant to be."

—**LISA BRECKENRIDGE**
Reporter/anchor Fox 11 News and *Good Day LA*

"A beautifully written prescriptive process for self realization, *Clarity* holds a powerful message and is a must-read."

—**DR. SHAILINDER SODHI**
President of Ayush Herbs, Inc. and
adjunct faculty member of Bastyr University

"As a physician, I have witnessed how emotions and thought patterns can determine our health and are a root cause of wellness or disease. Diane Altomare's book *Clarity* is a step-by-step guide that will help reveal which undesirable emotions, thoughts, addictions, and bad habits are affecting the health of your body and blocking your ability to perform at your highest state.

By utilizing her techniques, you will have the tools to transform your underlying feelings of fear, anger, and sadness into confidence, happiness, and fulfillment. I highly recommend this book for anyone wanting to discover the hidden and subtle emotional patterns which are preventing them from attaining their personal goals and peace of mind."

—ANDREW IVERSON, **ND**
Family practitioner and author of *Nature's Diet*,
Nature's Diet Cookbook, and *Nature's Detox*

CLARITY

CLARITY

Ten Proven Strategies to Transform Your Life

DIANE ALTOMARE

SelectBooks, Inc.
New York

This edition published by SelectBooks, Inc.
For information address SelectBooks, Inc., New York, New York.

First Edition

ISBN 978-1-59079-358-9

Library of Congress Cataloging-in-Publication Data
Names: Altomare, Diane.
Title: Clarity : ten proven strategies to transform your life / Diane
  Altomare.
Description: First edition. | New York : SelectBooks, Inc., [2016]
Identifiers: LCCN 2015012629 | ISBN 9781590793589 (pbk. book : alk. paper)
Subjects: LCSH: Self-acceptance. | Self-realization. | Adjustment
  (Psychology) | Change (Psychology)
Classification: LCC BF575.S37 A48 2016 | DDC 158.1--dc23 LC record
available
at http://lccn.loc.gov/2015012629

Book design by Janice Benight

Manufactured in the United States of America
10 9 8 7 6 5 4 3 2 1

Dedicated with love to Debbie Ford—your power, wisdom, and love graced my life in the most profound ways. I felt your presence in every word I wrote, and I thank you for your unconditional love—words can never express the depth of my gratitude for how you touched my life and guided me to find my dharma.

"Now, it's time to fly and create miracles!"

Contents

Foreword

SOMETHING IS STILL MISSING. We're working hard, we have more than we've ever had, and we have great access to the wisdom and inspiration of teachers and sages. Yet most people can't honestly say that they're truly happy. Even if you've accomplished some or all of your goals and dreams, you may be wondering "is this all?" I speak to hundreds of thousands of people a year, and I hear over and over again that they feel somewhat deflated or disillusioned because achieving their goals isn't bringing them the happiness and fulfillment they hoped it would.

In *Clarity*, my colleague Diane Altomare will show you how to move beyond this "disillusionment" and create the peace and fulfillment you deeply long for. You'll no longer be under the spell of thinking that you need to wait for the next big thing "out there" to bring you the happiness you're looking for.

Diane and I were introduced as a result of our deep connection to world-renowned speaker, author, and coach, Debbie Ford. Diane has spent the past fifteen years coaching thousands of people through Debbie's groundbreaking work on the shadow. I'm inspired by Diane's ability to profoundly and intuitively connect people to the root of their unhappiness, and heal themselves at their core.

It doesn't matter what's happened in your past or what you may be struggling with right now—with the powerful tools and insights in this book, you can create the life you want and feel amazing about yourself in the process.

Stop waiting for "someday when . . ." in order to experience deep fulfillment in your life. With Diane's revolutionary approach to living your life from the inside out, you will break through your limitations. Regardless of where you are in life, you can't help but feel greater peace, happiness, and fulfillment as you put into practice the powerful exercises, wisdom, and insights in this book. Enjoy!

—Marci Shimoff
New York Times best-selling author of *Happy For No Reason*
and the co-author of six Chicken Soup for the Soul books

Introduction

When someone walks into a room you immediately feel the totality of who that person is by the energy that he or she emanates. There is no denying the energy that we exude every day and in every situation. And yet most of us feel like we can cover up how we truly feel inside by the clothes we wear, the makeup we apply, the way we style our hair, or the cars we drive.

The truth is that who we are and how we feel shines through regardless of what we try to do to cover it up. We must work on the inside if we want to not only create amazing things in our life but also feel fulfilled, peaceful, and joyful at the same time. Eckhart Tolle says in *The Power of Now*, "If you get the inside right, the outside will fall into place."[1]

Unfortunately, this belief contradicts much of what our society worships and teaches. Look at Hollywood and think about celebrities. They often appear to be outwardly beautiful and successful, yet inwardly they have struggles just like everyone else. Often, the inner conflict they feel can be more intense than the average person because of the pressure to cover up how they truly feel inside, what's actually going on, and worse, the pressure to act like they have it all together.

Maybe you, along with tens of millions of people, were enraptured by the hit TV show *Friends* that has been popular for the past two decades.

Maybe you even had at one time or another, the popular haircut, called "The Rachel," that Jennifer Aniston made a household name.

Or maybe you were enthralled with the funny and quick witted "Friend" Chandler, played by Matthew Perry, who in real life appeared to have everything going for him including youth, fame, money, and success. Yet despite his outward success, Matthew Perry shared, "I was on *Friends* from age 24 to 34 and was in the white hot flame of fame. From an outsiders perspective it would seem like I had it all. It was actually a very lonely time for me because I was suffering from alcoholism. I think I was pretty good at hiding it, but eventually people were aware."[2]

And when singer and actress Demi Lovato spoke out about greatly admired actor Philip Seymour Hoffman's accidental overdose and she shared information about her own cocaine addiction as well. "Being a former addict, I physically and emotionally couldn't live without it—it was medicine to my pain," Demi said.[3]

And just like celebrities, who have two opposing extremes, there can be a huge disparity between how un-aligned our inner experience is with what our outward life looks like. In other words, how we feel may not be congruent with what our appearance, wealth, or status may portray.

This was all too familiar for me. I went to extreme lengths to cover up the pain and shame I felt as a child. On the outside, we looked like a normal middle class family. In fact, we had a brand new custom-built house. One day, some kid from school said, "Oh, so you live in *that* house?" He said it in amazement and awe of how lucky he thought I was. Unfortunately, the exterior facade of the house was so incongruent with what we were all grappling with and tortured by inside: Alcoholism—a brutal experience that renders you powerless and has you pretend that everything is okay when it's really a huge mess. What I truly wanted to say to that kid—more like scream at the top of my lungs—was the truth. I wanted to share the pain of what it was like to deal with (or more succinctly, suppress) the anger, shame, sadness, and disappointment I often felt.

I was so angry that I had to deal with attending AA meetings four nights a week as a family when all I wanted to do was be on the swings playing with my friends. However, through the secrets alcoholism breeds, I learned to hide my feelings, hide the truth, and hide what was really going on.

This is not an ordinary self-help book. *Clarity* is a declaration and a revelation that we, as a society, have become focused on the wrong things, and many of us are suffering silently inside because of it. The world of social media has only exacerbated our celebration of the facade. You can paint a beautiful picture on Facebook and Instagram, a false life and persona, when what is really going on in your home or in your heart may be devastating. Social media has heightened our obsession with "keeping up with the Joneses" and appearing as though we have it all together. Although nowadays, it is more like "keeping up with the Kardashians." Our focus is completely backwards, and we must start paying attention to what is happening. We as a society have been taught to value the exterior at any cost. To admire, emulate, and place the people who look the part of beautiful, successful, and happy on a pedestal and then try to live up to that illusion.

But the truth is that no matter how good things look on the outside, if we don't feel happy and at peace on the inside, it will never bring us what we desire.

Maybe you can relate to feeling so hopeless in some part of your life that you quit, give up, or feel resigned to simply accept it as it is. Maybe you wouldn't go to the extreme of taking your life or aren't battling alcoholism or drug addiction, but you know how it feels to go to extreme lengths to hide something painful that is going on inside of you. Perhaps you escape it with occasional drug or alcohol use. Or you turn to TV, food, or focusing on other people's lives instead of dealing with what's going on within you.

All too often when we feel stuck in life, we tackle the problem from the outside. We start a new exercise program or diet, we start taking a class, or we look for a new job. But where we should really start is with what we're feeling. With what's going on inside.

We can only pretend for so long. And in order to move beyond the facade we have created, we have to learn to feel and acknowledge what is truly going on. And that is why I'm writing this book. To share with you how to honor ALL of who you are, all that you've experienced and, most importantly, to not make yourself wrong for how you have responded to what has happened in your life. It is a natural and necessary reaction to respond emotionally to what we are facing in our life. It doesn't matter if you feel angry, sad, irritated, or depressed in response to what is happening. What matters is that you honor your feelings and allow yourself to have them.

Unfortunately, it took me twenty years to realize that the anger that I experienced as a child was a healthy emotion. The voice of my anger was simply trying to alert me and protect me.

In this book, I will guide you through the ten steps you need to take to start living your life from the inside out and will show you how to:

1. Identify what is holding you back from creating all that you desire in any part of your life.

2. Transform any negative emotion you may be feeling to a state of peace, grace, and compassion.

3. Stop transferring the pain or experiences from your past into your future and move beyond re-creating the same situations and circumstances in your life year after year

4. Stop allowing that negative voice within you to run the show and direct your life, telling you what you can and can't do.

5. Move beyond pointing the finger at the other person in your relationship and create true harmony within yourself and all your relationships.

6. Discover your default emotion and how it is secretly running your life and causing you to react inappropriately at inopportune times.

7. Give your emotions a voice and express them in a healthy way so they no longer control you or your life.

8. Truly let go of the past and embrace forgiveness instead of seeing it as something to be avoided at all costs.

9. Let go of the beliefs that are in opposition to what you truly want to create.

10. Make peace with the part of you that tells you, you're "not good enough," "don't have what it takes," or "are a failure."

11. And ultimately move beyond hiding from the past so you can use ALL of your experiences to create an amazing future, as well as powerfully give your unique contribution to the world.

How am I the perfect person to guide you through this process? Not only have I done the work myself to move beyond the pain of my past, but as a life coach for the past fifteen years, I have guided thousands of people, in private sessions, workshops, webinars, and speeches to let go of the pain of their past and create an inspiring and fulfilling future.

As shocking as it may seem, growing up in an alcoholic family was the perfect experience to guide me to the place where I could bring my greatest contribution to the world. Although it was difficult, challenging and extremely painful, on the flip side, the challenges of being in that very family, helped me develop some of the amazing parts of who I am. I became extremely intuitive, compassionate, and understanding of the pain other people are experiencing, and that is the reason that I can now hold a space for others to heal their past and create the life they truly want.

I traditionally work with the following four types of people (although I have worked with many others as well):

1. Adult children of alcoholics or adults who grew up with parents who were narcissists, depressed, or mentally ill.

2. The wife or husband who is hanging on and waiting to divorce their spouse when their youngest child graduates high school.

3. Women and mothers who have lost themselves and their identity and have given up on their hopes, desires and dreams.

4. Professionals that are ready to move to a career that is more aligned with who they are but aren't sure what this future position looks like.

In this book we will take on "whatever challenges or difficulties you are currently facing." I will guide you to create an exciting future that is aligned with what is most important to you and will show you how to feel amazing about yourself and your life in the process. Whether you feel stuck creatively, are unable to maintain a healthy relationship, feel depressed and lethargic, or are a people pleaser who is tired of always being last on the list, we will powerfully explore how to move past the pain you are experiencing. We will look at whatever may be going on inside of you that isn't congruent with what you want to create in your life and, more important, how you want to feel.

You will learn how to gracefully deal with whatever is going on inside of you so that you can create your reality the way that you want it to be. I'm here to tell you that you no longer have to white knuckle it, muscle through the pain, or cover up what's truly going on. You have the power to make a huge shift in your life right now and to stop repeating the same experiences over and over again. Let's begin by getting your inner world—the way you think, feel and see—to perfectly align with what you want to create and have in your life. Freedom, internal harmony, and true success await you.

The Steps and the Exercises

Each chapter of this book is called a "step." And each step includes both "Bite-size" exercises that can be accomplished in a short period of time and more in-depth exercises as well. There is also an exercise at the end of each step called a "process" that will require deeper reflection and will take a somewhat longer period of time to complete.

In addition, each step includes stories I call "client spotlights." Each story highlights a specific issue that my clients face and how they addressed that challenge, moved beyond it and ultimately created what they desired in their life. I also share my own stories in what I call "My Spotlight," in which I describe the challenges and conflicts in my life and how I resolved them.

This book is set up so you can complete all the steps and exercises in 10 weeks—if you choose to. However, given that we all have different methods of processing information and in addition have work, family, and other commitments, this time line is to be taken as a suggestion. I invite you to take as much time as you like for each step and not pressure yourself to move forward faster than you are able. Please enjoy a pace that is comfortable for you and that works for your personality and lifestyle. There is no rush. Transformation will come when you're ready for it.

CLARITY

Reconnect to Yourself

I've got it handled. Hey, listen world, I'M SUCCESSFUL! I scream success! I've got everything together! That is, UNTIL I walk into the familiar door of my home every night and actually feel what's really going on inside of me.

One of my clients shared that her evening ritual was comprised of "anything and everything I can use to escape my reality."

The minute I walk into the door and hear the garage close behind me, everything I was feeling, holding onto and pushing down during the day explodes like a volcano. As I drop my bag and sink into the couch, the thought of a glass of wine or a "guilty-pleasure" reality TV show to literally take me away to a different world is all that's on my mind.

Does this sound familiar? Maybe you seem to have it all together when you walk out your door in the morning, and yet in your deepest, most quiet moments, you know how untrue that really is. Maybe the truth is that you're struggling with something you feel like you have to cover up every day. Maybe this is something that happened a long time ago that you've convinced yourself doesn't really affect you anymore, or maybe it's a recent occurrence that you know is definitely playing with your emotions and dragging you down.

Perhaps you've been living this way since that traumatic experience five years ago, or maybe you've lived most of your life this way.

We all know what it feels like to cover up how we are feeling and put on a happy face. But for many of us, it has become our way of being.

I know all too well what it feels like to live this way, and that's why I'm here to share with you a radical new approach to living your life: From the Inside Out.

What exactly does it mean to "live from the inside out"? It means that how you feel inside is completely congruent with what you showcase to the world and that the beautiful smile that shines on your face in the morning when you walk out the door is actually how you feel inside. It means that your smile is authentic and isn't just something you plaster on your face every day to cover up the pain you feel inside. And it means that whatever pain you are feeling can be embraced and released so you don't have to continue to spend your life trying to cover it up.

As you read this chapter, ponder the following:

In your quiet moments, those moments when it's just *you*—maybe while you're driving, taking a shower, or late at night when everything has shut down for the day—does how you feel inside line up with what you showcase to the world? Is what you feel about who you are congruent with what you portray to everyone around you? Aren't you tired of continually managing and covering up what's truly going on within you?

You are not alone, and in the pages ahead, we are going to tackle this very issue and inner conflict that you are feeling. But for now, just sit with these questions as you begin to explore what it means to live your life from the inside out.

Upside Down

ALYSSA—A Mother Who Loses Emotional Control

Alyssa arrived on one of our coaching calls in a state of panic and proceeded to tell me the following story:

I was rushing around getting my son ready and asked him if he could get dressed, while I ran downstairs to find a few things we needed to take to school. We were running late, as we do most of the time. As I finally located the few things I needed, I quickly glanced at the clock. I immediately got frustrated, as it confirmed that we were late once again.

As I rushed up the stairs to get him, I found him playing; he hadn't even started getting ready yet. My mind was racing and I could feel that the emotions inside of me were about to erupt. I kept telling myself, relax, it's okay if we are late, stay calm. But there was a part of me that just didn't want to relax or stay calm and, unfortunately, that part of me won.

I picked up one of my son's toys and whipped it across the room, while screaming and yelling at him. He started to cry and looked back at me with shock, fear, and terror in his eyes. I just wanted to die. I couldn't believe I could do that to him. How could I have let this part of me take over? How could I have exploded like that on my sweet angel? He didn't deserve that. He didn't do anything to deserve that. I can still see him crying and how bad he felt about himself in that moment. I was so ashamed. I have to figure out a way to stop doing that.

I was so glad Alyssa had the courage to share that story with me. And we immediately began to dig deeper into what was going on in her life, what she was feeling, and what she had been trying to avoid. It was clear that squashing her emotions was no longer work-ing for her.

During our first few phone sessions, I guided Alyssa to identify the true cause of her anxiety and anger by calling up each emotion and connecting with the expression of that emotion. I shared with her that our emotions are our internal guidance system and each one holds useful insight. As she closed her eyes and connected with her feelings of anger and anxiety, she immediately realized that neither her anger nor anxiety had anything to do with her eight-year-old son. She was angry because she had let herself down. The more she allowed herself to feel the feelings that were present, she realized she was also frustrated and felt like her dreams and desires had all been pushed aside when she walked away from a lucrative and ful-filling financial career eight years ago to stay at home with her kids. It was tough for her to acknowledge this to herself and she shared how guilty she felt even bringing it up. After a few sessions of hon-oring her truth, connecting with her anger and anxiety, and working through the guilt she felt admitting how "unfulfilled and unaccom-plished she had been feeling," she breathed a huge sigh of relief. She was finally able to declare from a place of certainty and clarity that she wanted to go back to work part-time.

Fortunately for her, the company she worked for previously was looking for someone with Alyssa's experience to do consulting work a few times a week. Alyssa shared with me how she felt about her new position: "The moment I sat down at my desk, the first day at the office, I got a cup of coffee and turned on my computer, exhaled deeply and felt pure bliss." Alyssa's new balance of motherhood and working part-time was the perfect blend of being present for her kids and doing what she desired in her own life. She was beyond elated to be working again and felt fulfilled from all the new and exciting challenges and opportunities that were emerging.

As she put it, she was "truly happy again." And because she was happy again, she was able to bring those positive feelings to her kids.

Months later, we had a follow up phone session and I asked her how everything was going. She talked about how content and balanced she felt. She was more patient and loving with her kids, and even in the moments when things weren't lining up perfectly or the kids didn't listen, she was able to calmly direct them to do what was needed.

Insight About Alyssa

However, despite this success story, you may still be wondering how Alyssa could have reacted with such extreme anger toward her son. But I can tell you that in my coaching practice, I hear stories like this every day. I hear the stories of people who on the outside look like they have it all together, but behind closed doors, in the privacy of their own homes, they have unexpressed, suppressed emotions that are just waiting for a place to explode.

Unfortunately, most of us have been raised in a culture where expressing our feelings or being emotional is not always acceptable. We may be okay with having positive emotions, but we do not know how to properly express our negative ones. Our culture does not welcome uncomfortable feelings, expressions of true grief, sadness, despair, or anger, so we often cover up our real feelings by putting on a strong, pleasant facade. We have, unfortunately, been conditioned to believe that if we don't do this, we will be rejected or won't fit in. And because of this, we avoid these difficult emotions and, like Alyssa, try to push them away and ignore them. However, if we ignore them, if we don't allow them to move through us, they remain stuck within us and have nowhere to go. And worse, if they are not expressed and released, without knowing it, we create a ticking time bomb inside ourselves.

The good news is, however, that there is a solution. The solution is simple and is something within each one of us that we can access anytime we want to. Like Alyssa did in our session, one of the techniques you will learn is how to specifically identify what each one of your emotions is trying to express, where that emotion is coming from, and why you are reacting to situations in a certain way. Through this inner reflection, you will understand the purpose and guidance of each emotion and will gain the clarity you need to move forward in your life in a way that feels good to you.

The Importance of Self-Expression

Imagine eating your favorite piece of cake. You love the way it tastes and thoroughly enjoy the experience of eating it, but soon after it enters your body, you put a block on allowing that piece of cake to be digested and released. (Okay, I realize that consciously we can't do this, but just stay with me for a moment.) Now imagine eating this piece of cake every day for a year. And at the end of the year hundreds of pieces of cake have gone undigested. Imagine how you would feel. Maybe bloated, pent up, stuck, uptight, or even angry.

This is what happens when we don't allow ourselves to feel, express, and release our emotions. Similar to the piece of cake, we take in an experience or circumstance in our life. And as a result of that experience, we have a feeling about it. That feeling comes forth regardless of whether we allow ourselves to acknowledge it or not. (Emotions are much like thoughts; they unconsciously arrive without our assistance or help.) So now this feeling is present in our body. And if we don't allow ourselves to process, digest, express, and release it, that emotion remains stuck within us.

After years and years of eating these pieces of cake and not allowing them to be digested, we become chock full of undigested emotions and past experiences that we don't understand, didn't fully process, and probably aren't at peace with. One of the many downsides to this is that there is no more room for cake. There is no more room to create something new in our lives because we are all filled up. We are filled up with the past, with memories we are trying to avoid, and with limitations that keep us from creating the future we truly desire.

Most of us have a tendency to suppress our emotions. But we don't realize how many issues we are creating for ourselves by avoiding a simple emotion like sadness or anger. Our emotions are not the enemy; they are actually here for a reason. And they are helpful guides to let us know something is not quite right. If we can learn to feel our negative emotions, if we practice and get used to using our negative emotions as the insightful guides they are, these emotions can support us in understanding what changes we need to make to create an amazing life.

Throughout the next few chapters, you will learn ways to reconnect to yourself, honor what you are feeling, and identify more of what may be needed in your life. And in Step 6, you will learn a powerful technique to give your negative emotions a voice, called "The Emotional Expression Technique" which will help you move beyond any negative emotion and regain control over what you want to do in any moment of your life.

MY SPOTLIGHT

My "Not Good Enough" Self Is Born

I know all too well how difficult it is to feel and embrace negative emotions. Growing up in an alcoholic family created many experiences where negative emotions arose. In addition, I felt like I had to hide who I was and what was really going on. I masked our attendance of AA meetings four nights a week, at the age of eight, by telling my friends I couldn't play outside because we went out to eat all the time. I often felt humiliated and small and was overwhelmed with how someone else's problems could weigh so heavily on me. I was so burdened by it all that there were many times I desperately wanted to end it all—to make it all go away. I began to believe that I was the problem, that there was something wrong with me.

And I started to run away, piece by piece, one little part of me leaving at a time. Until I'd buried so much of myself that I really wasn't even there anymore. Somehow I felt responsible; if I could just be different or better or more lovable, the drinking would stop and everything would be okay. But it didn't stop and it wasn't okay for a very long time.

And throughout this internal struggle, my "not good enough" self was born. This part of me was born from the desperation of wanting to stop and somehow control the dysfunctional behavior of this alcoholic family. I decided it must be something I was or wasn't doing right. And that decision led me to determine that I wasn't lovable, there was something wrong with me, and I wasn't good enough. Because the pain of that was too much to bear, I set out on a path for decades to prove that "I was good enough" and everything would be okay.

In my attempt to prove I was "good enough" I did the following:

- Became an over-achiever
- Constantly pushed myself
- Set unrealistic expectations
- Strived for perfection
- Hid my imperfect self
- Had to be right and went to lengths to prove I was right
- Tried to get attention and approval
- Had to be the star of the show
- Covered up who I truly was
- Covered up what I was really feeling
- Felt bad about who I was
- Often tried to be someone else
- Always went above and beyond
- Gave more than I had to give
- Became the people pleaser
- Was always concerned with what others were thinking of me.

Everyone in a dysfunctional family suffers. Whether you are the person who has the issue or you are the one in relationship with that person, it doesn't matter. What matters most is being able to find yourself, your truth, and the journey back to who you are.

One day, during a long prom weekend, exhausted, strung out, and tired, I looked in the mirror, while everyone else was out in the living room being seventeen years old and partying without a care in the world, and something powerful came over me—my "good enough" self. She was finally here. I looked in the mirror and said out loud, "I'm too good for this. I can't do this to myself anymore. I don't deserve to treat myself like this."

And I made a decision right then and there in that moment to quit. To stop using mood altering substances to cover up the pain of feeling "not good enough," to stop trying to mask the pain of the part of me that was just trying to survive and make it through another day.

I was so glad to have found her . . . my good enough self. But I soon learned that my "not good enough self" was going to stick around. It wasn't such an easy habit to kick.

And that is where my journey with Debbie Ford began. Debbie unconditionally loved me, guided me, and taught me how to own my shadows and be at peace with myself and my past. Debbie's monumental work on the shadow taught me how to make peace with my "not good enough" self. And, most importantly, that there were many gifts that emerged from the part of me that didn't feel good enough.

The ultimate gift of this part of me was forever life changing and self-affirming. Because of the great pain in feeling not good enough, this part of me drove me to seek answers. My "not good enough" self drove me to the path of striving to improve and find peace with who I am. This path has directly led me to the most extraordinary journey back to my most powerful and authentic self as well as to spending the past fifteen years helping others heal and find peace with all of who they are. My "not good enough" self led me here, to this book and to this process.

Bottled-Up Emotions

Lydia—Exhausted and Depleted

When I first worked with Lydia, a forty-five-year-old attorney, she was exhausted and burnt out. She found herself getting angry often, had a short fuse, and felt cranky most of the time. This wasn't normal for her and she wanted to figure out what was happening and what she could do to feel happy again.

As we began to talk about what had been going on in her life, trying to identify where these negative feelings were coming from, she discovered that she was still angry about all the extra work she had to do over the past year with one of her children. Her teenage son had been acting out at school and doing drugs. Lydia had been in survival mode for the last twelve months, trying to get her son back on track and keep her family together in the midst of such trauma. She had overlooked the importance of really honoring her feelings and taking care of herself throughout the intense drama of the past year and was now feeling angry about how drained and empty the whole situation had left her.

Slowly, the more we talked, she began to discover that, for the entire year, she had almost completely disconnected from herself, her needs, and her feelings. She wasn't even aware that she had feelings other than the explosive anger that would erupt at moments, as she was just purely in survival mode. Everything had been about her son. The thoughts she had from morning to night were focused on what to do to help him, if it was her fault that his life turned out this way and how to respond appropriately to his latest debacle. He had been suspended from school for three days for fighting with another boy, and by this point she was consistently questioning herself and her ability to parent him effectively. As we began to delve more deeply into the anger she was experiencing, she started to become resistant to talking about it and, more importantly, feeling it.

Anger is a tough emotion for many of us to feel, and we've been conditioned to believe that anger is unacceptable. But remember, emotions simply come to us and we have to learn not to judge them. They are a natural part of being human. We have to learn how to feel them and release them. We may think we are doing ourselves a favor by ignoring our anger, but we aren't and unfortunately if we don't allow ourselves to feel angry and express it in a healthy way, it will erupt somewhere else down the road.

As I guided Lydia to connect with her anger, she began to see it as a tight black ball lodged in her abdomen.

"Now breathe into the anger and allow it to just be there, without trying to cover it up or make it go away," I said.

Lydia started to connect with the anger and allowed herself to feel it. Then I guided her to ask her anger, "What are you trying to communicate or express to me?" Even though she initially thought it was a bit crazy to talk to her anger, she followed my guidance and she received a profound message. Her anger told her that she was ignoring herself, diminishing her needs, trying to be Wonder Woman, and not allowing herself to receive love or care from herself or others. Instead, she was always taking care of everyone else.

As our session came to a close, I gave her some homework. Her work for the week was to express her anger in a healthy way. For the next seven days following her session, her assignment was to bring her anger on a daily walk and allow the anger to express what it needed to say. Yep, her work was to continue to talk to her anger and to see what it was trying to communicate with her.

Sure enough, when Lydia came to our phone session a week later, she couldn't stop talking about how much better and lighter she felt. She laughed as she told me about her walks with her anger. She said she actually felt like her anger wanted her to learn to pay more attention to herself and her needs. The anger told her to dedicate some time over the next few weeks to do whatever she wanted to do, especially to dedicate some time to doing things without any purpose attached, and to take time just for her. Lydia loved walks on the beach, having tea with her girlfriends overlooking the ocean and reading romance novels in her garden on a sunny day. She committed to beginning each one of those over the next few weeks. As Lydia continued to acknowledge her feelings, and reconnected to her desires over the next few weeks, her mood shifted and she felt happier and more at peace.

Insight About Lydia

Our emotions are not the enemy. They are signals and they are trying to tell us something. As we can see from Lydia's experience, her intense focus on caring for her emotionally distraught child caused her to ignore her feelings and go into survival mode. All the emotions she experienced during that year remained in her body and psyche and needed to be dealt with and digested. Remember, just because we may avoid feeling what is within us doesn't mean it's not present or will go away on its own. Avoiding or denying our true feelings leaves them in our body and psyche to be dealt with later, and it often makes dealing with the emotions worse because they've had a long time to build up.

If you take a moment, you can probably relate to holding in your feelings and then having them erupt somewhere they didn't belong. Maybe you know what it feels like to blow up at your spouse once you arrive home after a difficult day at work. Because your home is a safe space, you felt like the emotions that you were holding in all day, finally had a place to be released. Or perhaps you are unable to trust a new relationship you are in because of all the times you've been hurt in the past. Maybe you lash out at your current love interest because you expect he is going to mistreat you just like all those others before him. Or maybe you have a tendency to drive aggressively, overreacting to other drivers on the road, a classic case of road rage. No matter the situation, we all know that uncontrollable experience of a feeling that seemingly comes out of nowhere and is flung into the wrong situation or onto the wrong person.

Instead, we have the choice to consciously address what energy or emotion may be lingering from a previous experience before we enter into a new one. This is the only way to regain control of ourselves and become the director of our actions and our life.

EXERCISE

Your Turn: Talk To Your Anger

1. Sit quietly and comfortably for a moment in a chair or in bed propped up by pillows. You can do this for as long or as little as you like. I suggest that you allow at least fifteen minutes to give yourself some time to settle in. Say, "Hello anger . . ."

2. Take a deep breath and notice if you feel this anger in your body as a pit in your stomach, heaviness in your chest, or a weight on your shoulders.

3. Breathe into the anger and allow it to be there without trying to cover it up or make it go away. Take three slow deep breaths (each breath to the count of five) and just allow yourself to truly "feel" this feeling of anger.

4. Ask your anger, "What are you trying to communicate or express to me?"

5. Finally, ask your anger for one thing you can do today to express this emotion in a healthy way. Maybe take it on a walk and listen to the voice of this anger or write out the expression of your anger through journaling.

Your Emotional Wrapping Paper

It helps to picture each one of your actions wrapped up in some emotion. Maybe the emotion is appropriate to the situation, or perhaps it is something you are carrying over from an hour ago, yesterday or even last year.

Now imagine giving someone the gift of your time, and let's pretend that your "time" could be wrapped up in a box. See yourself meeting up with your friend for lunch. Imagine that in your hands you have your box of "time," and it has been beautifully wrapped with the energy of "love." See what this box looks like. Maybe it is wrapped in an exquisitely beautiful gold wrapping paper and has the most pristine white ribbon on top. When you give this gift of your time wrapped this way, you feel loving and the person who receives it feels loved.

Now imagine you show up to give the same gift of time, and instead of this beautifully wrapped box, your box is wrapped in black and red tattered wrapping paper that has tears and scratches all over it and has been so damaged that the box is now mangled. You are giving the same gift of your time, but the emotion you are sharing now may be anger or resentment. You feel angry and resentful as you give your time and the person receiving it feels that same anger and resentment you are sharing.

Although this is an imaginary scenario, it is helpful to visualize what you are wrapping your daily life and actions in. The emotion that you bring to each action pre-determines what will occur as a result. It's not just what we do that matters; it's the energy we bring to it that has much more of an impact on ourselves, others, and the end result. This is why it is so worth your time and energy to examine your emotions and clearly identify what they are here to teach you. When you can do that, you are able to receive the information you need and allow that emotion to move through you. And then you are free to move onto a new experience.

A Box of Love and Divine Validation

This past year on Mother's Day, my eight-year-old daughter gave me a small box that looked very similar to the one wrapped in love I was envisioning when I created and wrote the "Wrapping Paper" story that you just read. Keep in mind, that I had never heard the poem that was on this box before I wrote that story. The box she gave me had this beautiful silver pristine wrapping paper with hearts on it and was wrapped with a beautiful silver bow on top. It was the size of a ring box and attached to the bow was this letter:

This is a very special gift
that you can never see,
The reason it is special is
it's just for you from me.
Whenever you are lonely or feeling a bit blue,
you can hold this gift and know that I'm thinking of you.
You never can unwrap it,
please leave the ribbon tied
Just hold the box close to your heart for
it's filled with love inside.

And when she gave it to me on Mother's Day, I had tears streaming down my face and could hardly read through it to the end as I was so choked up. It was so touching and memorable, of course, because it was coming from my sweet, precious daughter. And in addition, it was divine validation, because in my hands, I had received something that was the physical form of a story I had created and written two years prior to my daughter handing me this gift.

Emotional Freedom

In order to be truly free to create something new in our life, we must first look within to see what lingering emotions need to be digested. Then, we need to learn how to feel our emotions and not suppress them. We can absolutely learn how to do this by allowing our emotions to be as they are in the moment, so they don't build up and cause us pain in the future. And once we learn to identify what pain or issue is rearing its ugly head, we can move past repeating the same situation or pattern over and over again and create the future we truly desire.

This book will help you do just that. It is a ten-step process to living from the inside out. We live in a constantly moving, changing, distraction-oriented society. When is the last time you sat down and actually paid attention to how you were feeling? Are you happy? Has your life turned out the way you wanted? Are there areas where you are dissatisfied? Do you want to do something about that?

You may not know the answers to all of these questions, and that's okay. The work in this book will help you rebuild your life from the inside out. That means you are going to tackle what's currently going on within you. Throughout the steps and exercises, you will become reconnected to yourself and to the part of you that knows what you actually want and need to be happy, fulfilled, and to feel truly alive.

As you have already explored, learning to feel is one of the ways you can reconnect to yourself. Another powerful way to reconnect is through silence, solitude, or stillness of any kind. The noise in our lives, in our thoughts, in our home, and on TV keeps us disconnected from ourselves. The busier we are and the more we jam pack into our schedule and in our lives, the more disconnected we often become. Connecting to a place where we are able to just sit and be with whatever we are feeling is a necessary practice to cultivate if we want to truly be at peace in our life. Think about this. How often do you just sit and do nothing? Do you specifically schedule in quiet time for yourself on a daily walk or with a cup of tea, gazing out the window? Or are you and your needs an afterthought?

I have found it to be a necessary practice to simply sit quietly and allow myself to reflect on whatever is taking place in my life on any given day. Sometimes I'll do this for twenty minutes, and at other times, I will take a quick five-minute block of time to regroup between projects or calls. It's a time to become aware of where I am and how I am feeling about whatever happened that day.

Some people find it useful to journal the thoughts and feelings that are coming forth. I prefer to allow this time to just be a free space of time where I don't have to write or do anything. It can be simply a time to allow everything to download and move through me instead of having another "to do," such as journaling. However, whatever feels right to you, is vital for you to do. Taking time each day to identify how you are doing and how you are feeling during this time of inner reflection is essential to maintaining this deep connection with yourself on a long-term basis.

As you take more time for this reconnection and begin to practice "feeling" your emotions instead of pushing them aside, you may feel that you have more control over identifying what is going on in your life and why you actually feel the way you do. Identifying your emotions and allowing yourself to feel them as they are is an essential step in the healing process. As we feel our emotions and allow them to be as they are, they can easily move through us and be released.

When we suppress our emotions and don't see the wisdom or guidance in them, we become stuck right where we are, preventing growth and healing. And more often than not, the result of avoiding our feelings and what is truly going on in our life causes more issues. In the process, we create more drama and chaos in our lives, because we are transferring our negative emotions to places, people, or situations where they don't belong. The next chapter will help you identify how that may be happening for you.

Take some time right now to reconnect to yourself and complete the exercises at the end of this chapter. Your reconnection to yourself will ensure your ability to feel your emotions and open up to the guidance they are here to give you. And, ultimately, it will allow you to feel more connected and at peace.

Bite-Size Exercise

❖ ❖ ❖

Take a moment right now to choose something you enjoy that would help you reconnect to yourself over the next few days. Maybe it's yoga, a quiet walk of solitude, sitting in nature, meditating, or just gazing out the window with a cup of tea. Schedule it in your calendar now and give yourself this gift of reconnection.

Want More? Listen as I guide you through the exercise below on audio. Find the "Reconnection" audio at www.dianealtomare.com/Reconnection

THE RECONNECTION PROCESS

Find a time within the next few days to dedicate ten minutes to the following exercise. Turn off your phone, go somewhere comfortable, and allow yourself to focus on reconnecting with yourself.

1. Take a deep breath and close your eyes, and as you do, focus your energy on what is going on within you.

2. As you take another deep breath, notice where in your body your breath is most present. Do you feel it grounded low in your abdomen or is it higher in your chest? Just notice where in your body, you feel your energy and breath.

3. Watch your breath and notice that with your focus and attention on your breath, you can gently move your breath two inches behind your navel to ground your breath in your abdomen. Grounding your breath helps you to get into deeper connection with yourself.

4. As you allow yourself to get into this deeper connection, just breathe into this present moment, as it is.

5. On your next breath, take a moment to observe anything that is getting in the way of you being totally connected to your breath. Maybe your thoughts are taking you away from focusing on your breath or maybe there is an emotion present that is keeping you from being connected to both your breath and yourself.

6. For a moment, follow that thought or emotion. Notice where it is taking you and just go with it. Maybe it is connecting you with an experience from earlier today or something in the past that you don't feel good about.

7. Allow yourself to breathe into the emotion or experience and notice what that feels like in your body. Do you feel tightness in your chest? A lump in your throat? Maybe there is sadness in your heart. Take some time to breathe deeply into whatever area that emotion or experience is connected to. And just allow it to be there.

8. Take a deep breath and ask this emotion for guidance. Breathe into the part of your body where you feel this emotion and ask, "What are you (the emotion) trying to express?" "What are you trying to communicate to me?" Maybe your anger is here to let you know a boundary has

been crossed. Or your guilt is letting you know that you don't feel good about something that has happened. Take as long as you need to deeply connect with this emotion and listen for the wisdom this emotion has for you.

9. On your next breath, ask this emotion to give you a healthy way to express it. What could you do over the next few days to give this emotion a healthy expression? Do you need to journal about how you are feeling? Maybe you need to take this anger kickboxing, take your grief to yoga, or your anxiety on a walk. Trust the answer you are receiving and schedule it in your calendar.

Understand What's Really Going On

Imagine walking into your favorite coffee shop to meet one of your friends, and as you sit down, you lift a large heavy sack over your shoulder and fling it onto the table. This sack is old, extremely worn, and outdated. When your friend arrives, she slumps into the chair next to you and her oversized, antiquated bag lands at her feet. As you both share the events of your week, you begin to take things out of your bag and give them to each other. You begin to "transfer" your fears, worries, concerns, and limitations from the past into your current experience. Without even noticing, you both transfer all of this "baggage" into your conversation.

Your conversation sounds something like this: "I think my husband is cheating," you say. Although you aren't certain he's having an affair, you delve into a long explanation about the signs you've seen and how you feel: "I'm not sure he is, but something just doesn't feel right. He's just not interested in anything I say anymore, and he's making excuses to stay out after work a lot lately, and I noticed that he's changed the password on his phone."

Being both empathetic and compassionate, your friend wants to be able to relate to your experience and share her "wisdom" with you. So she reaches into her bag of relationships, as coincidentally she has had this exact experience and knows what it feels like. She takes it out of her bag and shares her wound with you, "Oh Gina, you better be careful. I went through that and it was awful! That's exactly how I found out, too—I saw her name on his phone."

Now, remember, because of the specific experience she had in the past, your friend is assuming that your husband is definitely being unfaithful and that you're going to experience the exact same pain and hurt she did. In this moment, her past, her wounds, and her limitations are being transferred to you. And at the same time, this conversation may be bringing up the unresolved feelings she has about her past relationship. So when she talks to you about your experience, she doesn't have the ability to see your situation differently from hers. In this very moment, her past may cloud your future, if you are unaware of what is taking place.

What is actually happening is a form of transference, which was first described by psychoanalyst Sigmund Freud and is the basis of what we will be exploring in this chapter. Transference is simply the continuation of some way of being from our past, often from our childhood relationships, into our current situation and relationships. It is literally the way we transfer the past into our current experiences month after month and year after year.

Conversations like this happen every day. We sit down with our friend for a cup of tea and she casually shares something she's struggling with. Then without thinking, we dive into our own expertise to offer advice, comfort, and support. Although we may mean well, if we haven't fully healed from something that wounded us in the past, we won't be able to view her situation with clear eyes. Whatever emotional wounds we have that aren't healed skew the way we see and interpret new situations. They are literally the lens through which we view what is possible. The end result of this is that we transfer our wounds and fears onto other people without even noticing what's going on.

Transference Can Limit Our Possibilities

Transference appeared in the coffee shop story in two ways: First, your friend transferred her unresolved hurt, wounds, and feelings from the breakup of her marriage to the way she interpreted your relationship issues. Second, she allowed her feelings around being abandoned by her ex-husband and her difficulty trusting others to ultimately affect the advice she gave you.

The obvious problem with this friend-to-friend exchange and transference, in general, is that it has the potential to limit our possibilities. In order to follow our own path and grow into who we are meant to be, it is essential to acknowledge that we each have our own journey. Your reasons for being in your relationship, as well as the lessons you need to learn, will be different than hers, even if they have some similarities. The one glaring difference, however, is that you have to work through your relationship and it has nothing to do with her past, what she experienced, or how her marriage ended.

Think about all the times that you sit down with this friend or she sits down with you. You start a somewhat innocent conversation about what's happening in your life. And before long, the stories of the past are being transferred back and forth. And worse, the limitations from the past are being projected into the future through a casual conversation, just like this one.

As I discussed in Step 1, our inability to feel and express our emotions keeps us from being open to new experiences and possibilities for our life. Fortunately, by using the tools from Step 1, you can now begin to more powerfully honor and embrace those difficult emotions so that you can learn from them and move on. However, there is still work to do with the experiences from the past that are holding us back from what we desire. Those unhealed wounds often reappear when we encounter an experience that feels similar to something that occurred in the past.

Avoiding or denying the emotions that are connected with that past event prevents us from seeing ourselves and what we are currently experiencing in the proper light. Those previous experiences are still with us and, worse, are tainting our ability to embrace the uniqueness of what is taking place now. For example, when your friend used her painful experience as a point of reference, she potentially changed the way you viewed the challenge with your husband. We do this to ourselves all the time in different ways without recognizing that it's happening. You now have the opportunity to move beyond limiting yourself in this way.

The Transference Box

Remember the Emotional Wrapping Paper Story from Step 1? Just as we transfer our emotions and energy to each other, we also transfer our past into our future through a similar transferring of energy. We are going to call this "The Transference Box."

You can use the visual of this "Transference Box" to identify what you may be transferring from the way you feel about yourself to the person you are sitting across from, what you are transferring from the relationship you had with your mother or father to your spouse or what beliefs you are transferring from previous generations to future ones.

Just imagine that when you were young that box was tinier than a small ring box and wasn't filled up with much.

And then year after year, the situations and experiences that you didn't know how to process, resolve or deal with, became tucked away in this box.

As you have experienced life and made decisions about who you are and what you can and can't do, you have added issues, beliefs, and limits on yourself and have also added them to this box. That small tiny ring box may now be the size of an overstuffed piece of luggage ripping at the seams and lugging within it the weight of your past.

By consciously choosing to become aware of what's in this transference box, you can regain control over your life and begin to make conscious decisions about what you actually want to bring into your current circumstances and what you are ready to let go of and move beyond.

One of my private clients recently shared with me that she never knew all of this stuff was holding her back until she began her coaching sessions. She was amazed at how many unresolved emotions were lingering from what happened to her several years ago. And she shared that she was feeling like a totally different person now that she had learned how to truly embrace those feelings and let them go.

You too, can consciously sift through that box and decide what you are ready to let go of and what contents are worthy of keeping.

This transference box, filled up with your memories, experiences and unresolved issues may still be closed after forty years. Maybe you haven't opened it up to sift through it and decide what serves you and what you want to let go of. Maybe you feel like you are still living within the confines of that filled up, overflowing box and the restrictions of the past. And maybe you are transferring the negative experiences in there to your adult relationships and experiences. It's just what organically happens. You become a combination of all the experiences that you've had, both good and bad, until you consciously work through them, process what has happened and begin to make different choices.

In order to really grow and evolve into who you are meant to be today and in the future, you will want to open up that box and allow yourself the freedom to move beyond the confines of the contents of that box and expand into a whole new evolution of yourself.

Reactions From the Past

The second step in the process of living from the inside out is to identify what's *really* going on and understand what experience from your past is causing you to react, respond, or act in ways that don't serve you. After reading this step, you will understand how you are transferring the past into your present experience and relationships. You will also see why we as human beings recreate the same situations and circumstances in our lives year after year, even though we so desperately want to create something different. And, most importantly, you will learn to identify what you need to do to make peace with and heal from the negative experiences of the past so you can create what you truly desire.

I would like to invite you to explore a whole new possibility for yourself. Examining your past doesn't have to be an excruciating or difficult experience. Yes, that's right—I said it. The process of exploring unresolved events from your past can actually be eye opening, freeing, and even exciting at moments. How is this possible? By realizing that it's often more difficult to carry these ineffective or destructive ways of being around year after year, desperately wanting something different and not being able to create it.

Even so, you may still feel uneasy about delving into your past. I understand why. Many times, I hear people say, "I don't want to go back there or deal with what happened that long ago." But it is essential to understand how we are continuing patterns and ways of being in our life that we learned early on because we can't change what we don't acknowledge. We may think we are furious with our spouse and try to fix our marriage or relationship, but often this very relationship is mirroring a relationship we had in childhood with a parent or sibling.

The true healing, then, is in the recognizing and making peace with the "original" relationship that caused us pain. Fortunately, we can do this without the other person being involved. And once we do, we can then make peace with our current circumstances and have the freedom to make the changes we desire.

Kathryn—No Time For Herself

When Kathryn arrived at our first coaching session, I could tell immediately that she was in a state of desperation by the panicked tone of her voice. As we began exploring why she might be feeling this way, she quickly identified the frustration she felt about how much time she spent focused on making other people happy. What upset her most about this was that she had little to show for it. She was in a marriage that wasn't working, had a job she didn't like, and felt unfulfilled and miserable most of the time. Although she had many people who loved her—and loved that she shared her time, focus, and attention with them—at the end of the day she felt alone and unfulfilled.

Kathryn shared that she never had time for herself and was always rushing to be by someone's side, whether it was for a spur of the moment shopping trip or to support a friend "in need." I knew that it was likely that Kathryn had developed this pattern much earlier in life. As we talked, she began to open up about what her childhood was like.

She said that as a result of her parents' divorce, she spent many days after school by herself in an empty, quiet house. As she continued to tell her story, she voiced, "Even though I feel like we are onto something, I am hesitant and uncomfortable revisiting the memories of being home alone. It is something I have worked hard to forget."

I assured her that it would be highly beneficial for her to do this and would open up a whole new way of looking at her life. Hesitantly, Kathryn allowed herself to identify with and connect with that little girl and view her life through this little girl's eyes. As she did, she began to see that it was this very past that was causing her to react in ways that were leaving her exhausted and unfulfilled. She was beginning to understand why she would drop her own needs and run to someone else's rescue when they needed something. And why even the smallest requests from other people became more important than tending to her own needs.

She recognized that her need to do anything to be with people and take care of them was present because she didn't want to be alone and, even more significantly, didn't want to "feel" alone like she did as a child. Kathryn was initially shocked that her fear of being alone as a child was still present in her adulthood and how much it was controlling her decisions. But as she began to embrace her feelings and the little girl who was home alone every day after school, she began to connect the dots and understand why her past was still present in her life.

During the course of our coaching sessions, Kathryn made great strides in learning how to stop letting the fear of being alone direct her future. She learned to put her needs first and realized that she could say no to people and would even be okay if she were alone.

Insight About Kathryn

When Kathryn first came to me, she couldn't understand why she was so exhausted and unfulfilled in her life. She felt that if other people would just stop demanding so much from her, she would feel better. But through the course of our work together, she saw that it wasn't other people creating her reality and that the changes she needed to make could only come from within.

By identifying, acknowledging, and owning that we play a significant part in all of our relationships and in any situation in our life, we take back our power and have the energy to make the changes we desire. Even though it is often easier to blame others for the way they are reacting or responding to us, the only person we can change is ourselves. The work of digging deep, often into the uncomfortable experiences of our past, helps us understand why we act the way we do and opens us up to new possibilities for our future.

Only *You* Can Heal the Wounds of Your Past

It is important to clarify that taking responsibility for or looking at our part in the co-creation of our life, doesn't necessarily mean it was our fault. This is an important distinction to make. You may have had traumatic things occur in your past that left wounds in place that are causing you to attract negative energy or recreate painful experiences over and over again.

But there is one important realization we all must come to at some point in our lives, if we are going to change our future circumstances. Regardless of how difficult our past experiences have been, we are the only ones who can heal the wounds of our past and create something new. The greatest gift we can give ourselves is to look at how any patterns or reoccurring situations in our relationships are similar to the ones of the past so we can face them and heal them once and for all. Rather than allowing ourselves to simply suffer from the pain of a breakup or a relationship that isn't working, we can use each relationship to guide us to a place of healing and, ultimately, to a deeper relationship with ourselves and others. The end result is a feeling of being more in control of our current experiences and having more freedom to create what we desire in our life.

There are many ways that we transfer our childhood experiences into our adult life. One of them is from a parent or sibling to our spouse. But we also transfer these experiences or "play out" our wounds from childhood with our in laws, co-workers, friends, and children.

MY SPOTLIGHT

Negativity Weaves Through My Relationships

This next story illustrates how I struggled for an entire decade with the same issue before being able to heal my hurt and pain.

I was so thrilled to have been nominated for Homecoming Court senior year in high school. Each member of this court was vying for the one spot of Homecoming Queen. Back in high school, being the Homecoming Queen was a big deal. And the events leading up to the whole school voting for who would be chosen were also a big deal. One of those events included being announced as one of the members of the Homecoming Court on the loudspeaker in the gym during a school assembly. I still remember the dress I wore on that day. It was a silk green dress and I proudly displayed the sash across my chest that said "Homecoming Court."

As my name was called and I walked through the middle of the gym with the entire school watching, a few girls booed at, what seemed to me, the top of their lungs. If there was anyone in the gym clapping, I certainly couldn't hear it. Although I knew there were many people who were rooting for me, the only ones I heard that day in the gymnasium were the girls who hated me—the girls who were booing. I thought I was going to die. Although I knew who the girls were because they used to be my best friends, and I understood that they were booing me because we had been battling superficial teen-age girl stuff for months, it didn't lessen the impact that moment had on me for a whole decade.

From that moment forward, the shame I felt in that gym, coupled with other unresolved issues I was holding onto, caused me to hide and disappear in my life. I turned to many different vices to numb my pain and to hide the feeling that there was "something wrong with me" and that it wasn't safe to "shine my light."

That one moment of shame in that high school gymnasium remained with me for years, and I transferred it into my life from that point forward, in many ways. One was to diminish my great-ness and gifts. But the one I want to highlight here is how it affected all my relationships with female friends and female family members. I decided in that moment that women weren't to be trusted. That even if they were once your friends, they would always turn on you. And so I became the girl who loved to have guy friends. I became the girl who didn't have many close girlfriends and who certainly didn't trust women in a work setting or in any other place.

Although I avoided closeness in relationships for many years before finally dealing with this pain, there came a point in my life when I chose to no longer hide behind it. It became more painful to hide than to deal with the feelings I was avoiding and move past them. By finally facing the hurt that occurred that day and working through my feelings, I was able to open up to healing that wound and experiencing something new. It wasn't easy, and it took years to embrace the shame and embarrassment I felt about it and to discover how to make peace with it.

However, when I was truly able to feel those feelings as they were and love myself through it, I was able to let go of all that I had attached to that experience and set myself free. By doing this inner work and healing, I no longer had to hide, avoid female friendships, or re-create that past. I was now free to choose differently by assuring myself it was safe to trust again. As a result, today I am able to create and have relationships with female friends again.

Now, if I feel insecure with one of my girlfriends, I know that this past event is simply rearing its head. The power and freedom I have in knowing what is happening is amazing. It means that I don't need to create drama or chaos in my current female friendships because of a past hurt. Instead, I know how to honor myself and my feelings and have compassion for the pain I experienced at the age of seventeen. I have the confidence now to take care of myself in any situation where that old hurt may re-appear. I am now self aware and confident enough to understand how and what to do to care for myself and not allow the negative opinions of a few outweigh how I feel about myself.

My best friend knows all about this experience, and because I'm at peace with it now, we can joke about it. She'll say, "Don't go high school on me," which I always laugh at and interpret as her love for me, because she has the same fear. She has her own version of "the fear of being rejected" by someone she loves. And she has experienced how that fear shows up in her current relationships. Because we have this understanding of each other's pain, past, and experiences, we have a great depth of compassion and love present in our friendship.

With this one tool, you can create so much freedom in your relationships and your life. Both in the freedom you will have to be who you are with all your strengths, talents, fears, and doubts and the space you can create for everyone else in your life to be all of who they are. In Step 4, we will expand our conversation of transference and you will learn how to specifically identify how the past may still be present in your romantic relationships. It is, by far, one of the most powerful tools you can embrace. By being conscious in your relationships and knowing when you are transferring the wounds of your past, you can consciously create a deeper connection and share a greater depth of who you are with the people in your life.

The Deep Roots of the Past

CLIENT SPOTLIGHT

Samantha—Childhood Pain Transfers to Marriage

Samantha grew up in an alcoholic family. As alcoholics often do, her father drank during the day and into the night. As we explored her experience, she shared that she remembered it as if it were just yesterday, even though almost two decades had passed. What she most remembers as a little girl is hearing the bar door creak open in the middle of the night. What always followed the creaking of that door was the sound of ice cubes clinking in the glass. She remembers feeling immediate terror and fear, knowing what those sounds meant. Those sounds began the change in her father from a loving, caring man to a distant, distracted person who rejected her and her needs. As a result, she felt insecure and felt a lack of safety when he was drinking.

Fast-forward twenty-five years to her current life with her husband who likes to drink a few times during the week. Although he doesn't display the signs of alcoholism or the intensity of her alcoholic father, he has similar behavior. The important part of this connection is not that her husband is exactly like her father. But that when her husband does certain things, it reminds Samantha of her Dad and her childhood. More importantly, because these wounds haven't been healed completely, it evokes the feelings of insecurity and fear she had as a child. It unconsciously brings her right back to the age of eight years old.

So when Samantha hears her husband in the kitchen in the evening and the ice cubes clinking in the glass, the little eight-year-old girl inside of her immediately reverts to a place of panic and fear. Until Samantha can heal this little girl's fears and insecurities, she will continue to transfer her childhood feelings onto her husband and her marriage. That little girl's fear and insecurities were unconsciously tucked away in her transference box and are now reappearing in her relationship. The problem with this is that getting upset with her husband for drinking won't ever resolve this issue within her. Even though his drinking is triggering something from her past, getting upset with him and trying to handle her wounds with him won't help her heal.

What Samantha needs to focus on is using this as an opportunity to acknowledge that the little eight-year-old girl needs healing. The little girl within her needs to be acknowledged for her fears and insecurity. She needs to be reassured that Samantha is no longer eight years old and can learn new ways to take care of herself, unlike when she was a child.

During our phone coaching sessions, Samantha learned how to deeply connect with the little girl within her that felt insecure and scared, which I will show you specifically how to do in Step 3. She learned the specific needs of this child and exactly how to comfort her in the moments she was feeling unsafe or affected by her husband's drinking. And she became really good at not transferring the feelings of this little girl into her marriage, which will be much easier for you to apply to your life as well, once you gain clarity on how you may be transferring the past into your current experience.

Insight About Samantha

Even though Samantha's husband's drinking still made her uncomfortable at times, she knew exactly what to do to take care of herself in those moments and how to comfort the little girl within her. Because of these specific techniques, she no longer panicked when he was drinking at parties, like she did in the past. And because her husband was aware of how his drinking brought up her past, instead of getting defensive when she talked to him about it, he was understanding and compassionate. As a result of their deeper understanding of each other, they felt more connected and loving towards each other. He began coming home earlier from work, excited to see her again and they started going on dates once a month to rekindle their romance.

The Little Child Within

You may have noticed that in both Kathryn and Samantha's stories they had to learn to connect with the little girl from the past who was still controlling the actions of their grown women selves. The fact is that much of transference comes from childhood wounds. Now that you are taking the time to identify what is *really* going on in each situation, in the next step, you will learn how to connect with the little child within you who so desperately wants to be heard.

But first, use the following exercises to identify what experiences from the past may still be limiting you.

Bite-Size Exercise

❖ ❖ ❖

Use what you learned from this step over the next few days. Notice how you may be transferring the past into your current experiences by observing the moments when reoccurring feelings are present or when you are experiencing the same unresolved situation again. Then honor yourself by simply acknowledging what is surfacing from the past. And affirm for yourself that you won't always feel like this, as you are in the process of learning new ways of experiencing your life.

Want More? Download a transference worksheet at www.dianealtomare. com/Transference

The Transference Process

Find a quiet place to do this visualization. Close your eyes and take a couple of slow deep breaths. As you follow your breath inside, observe any thoughts or emotions that may try to get in the way of this simple connection to your breath. And when this happens, just gently refocus your attention on your breath again, as you gain clarity through this exercise.

1. Identify an area of your life that you don't feel good about. For example, this might be your career, your home life, your relationship, your weight or health, and so on.

2. Take a deep breath and connect with the feelings that you are feeling about this part of your life or about an event that recently occurred. Just breathe into these feelings. For example, I feel angry, sad, frustrated, out of control, or powerless.

3. Take a deep breath and allow yourself to see the event before you as if you are the observer—you are observing it outside of yourself. Notice your role in this interaction. Did you feel out of control or were you trying to control something? Did you hold back expressing yourself and then blow up in anger and frustration? As you observe what happened, notice how this feels to you?

4. Take a deep inhale and notice if this is a familiar feeling or experience for you. Have you felt this way before and when? In your adult life or as a teenager or child? Was there another time in your life when you felt this out of control, sad, or powerless?

5. On your next breath, notice what you may be transferring from the past into this situation, event, or relationship. For example, if you felt out-of-control as a child, you may be trying to control everything and everyone around you. Or if your needs weren't met or you weren't heard as a child, you may be transferring your need to be heard and honored into what you're experiencing. Maybe you felt alone as a teenager, and it's showing up now as you being needy or always bringing attention to other people's opinions or views of you. Just acknowledge whatever you may be seeing as a result of this exercise.

6. Take a moment now to visualize that child or teenager and the age she was when she felt those feelings. Connect with this child who is still showing up in your life by transferring these feelings into your current experience. Tell this child that you are here now, as the adult, to protect her, listen to her and keep her safe. As you begin to develop a new relationship with this child, she will trust you to take care of her needs instead of feeling she has to handle everything with her immature approach. Let this child know that you

are going to walk with her, hold her hand, and check in with her often this week.

7. Finally, ask yourself, "What action can I take over the next few days to find peace within myself regardless of what is happening? What is one thing I can do to nurture myself and acknowledge how I am growing as a result of this very experience and what is one thing I can say to myself to remind myself of this growth?" Make sure to schedule your actions in your calendar and put your reminder in your phone or computer.

Embrace Your Inner Child

Do you ever wonder why grown adults act childish at times? Maybe you've witnessed it in one of your relationships, as you've watched someone storm out of a room, throw a tantrum, or snap at you abruptly. Maybe it's happened to you in that moment when you just couldn't figure out why you reacted so intensely to what your friend or sister-in-law said.

Most of the time when we "act out" in ways that seem inappropriate or immature, we are not "acting out" from our adult self, but the little girl or boy within us is responding or reacting to what's happening. No matter how old we are, or how evolved we strive to be, we are all truly "kids at heart," and there is a little child within each of us who still has challenges, desires, and needs.

As we saw in Kathryn's story in the previous chapter, it wasn't until she learned to connect with who she was as a little girl, and embrace the feelings, she had at that young, impressionable age, that she was able to see how those same fears and feelings were driving her adult life. Because she had never allowed herself to fully feel those uncomfortable emotions of fear and sadness, they were still present. And although she wasn't aware of it, those unresolved experiences were still controlling her and her life.

We all experience this at some point in our lives. And in this step, you will have the opportunity to connect with your inner child by listening to what he or she wants to communicate to you as well as learn what this inner child most fears. This very connection will enable you to move past whatever limitations you may be facing in your life and relationships, so you can stop letting those fears drive you.

This step is so crucial to living from the inside out because so often we are letting our little girl and little boy selves run the show. It's time now to allow them to be heard and move beyond that way of being in the world.

Loving Your Inner Child

It's important to note that our inner child is neither good nor bad; he or she is perfect just as they are. And finding unconditional love and acceptance for this child is our ultimate goal. It is simply our job to acknowledge this child and listen to his or her needs, hopes, and desires, as well as to love this child, regardless of whether they are acting out or not.

In addition, it is important for us, as the adults, to give them the attention and care they are so desperately seeking; otherwise they will continue to be in the driver's seat in our lives, trying to get their needs met in a host of destructive or ineffective ways. Think of your inner child as a real child that you would parent. We still "love" our children even when they are causing havoc or being destructive. Our own inner child needs the same care and attention that we would give one of our children.

John Bradshaw talks about this way of loving ourselves in *Healing the Shame that Binds You*. He states that "The job of parents is to model. Modeling includes how to be a man or woman; how to relate intimately to another person; how to acknowledge and express emotions; how to fight fairly; how to have physical, emotional and intellectual boundaries; how to communicate; how to cope and survive life's unending problems; how to be self-disciplined; and how to love oneself and another.[4]

Perhaps you didn't receive this guidance or this expression of love as a child. However, you have the opportunity now, as an adult to take care of and protect your inner child from this point forward.

Jenny—Feeling Hopeless about Romance

When Jenny arrived at our first coaching session, she was feeling desperate about her romantic life. She was forty-five years old and had a successful graphic design business, but had two failed marriages behind her. She shared with me how badly she wanted to make her current relationship work and unfortunately it was in shambles. I asked her to share more about what was presently happening.

"I just don't get it. I was so into him in the beginning, and now I feel like every time we get together, we fight. It always ends up with me quickly packing my things and leaving. I think we've sort of broken up again for the fifth time now, but I really miss him. He is the only man that I'm really interested in. No one else makes me feel the way he does, but we just don't seem to be able to make things work."

You can probably guess that transference was present in Jenny's relationship, because it was an issue that was popping up again and again. She was simply transferring a previous way of being from a past relationship into this one. And one of the ways it was showing up in this relationship was in her need to quickly flee when things were uncomfortable. Once we knew that transference was present, connecting with her inner child was the next step.

I asked Jenny to share information about her childhood relationships. The first relationship she told me about was with her dad. She shared that he left when she was only four years old. I asked her to close her eyes and see herself as that little four-year-old girl. I explained to her that we were going to look at the experience of her dad leaving through the perspective of this little child.

Although she didn't remember him leaving, she began to get choked up as she shared the details of it from this little girl's heart. "I remember wondering why the other kids at school had their dads at assemblies and plays and I didn't. I remember my mom being sad most of the time. I remember the few times he came over, I just wanted to jump in his lap and have him hold me. And mostly, I remember crying for hours when he didn't."

This was the first time Jenny had ever connected with this little girl's feelings as an adult. She was beginning to see a glimpse of the impact this had on her life and her relationships, even though her way of dealing with it was to tough it out and never talk about it.

Insight About Jenny

By connecting with her Inner Child, Jenny realized that her inability to remain in a relationship when things became difficult was directly related to what she experienced as a little girl. It was now obvious to her what a huge impact it had on her life. She had been carrying the feelings of being left and abandoned by her dad for more than forty years. Her fear of being abandoned caused her to always jump the gun and make sure she was the one who left first. This was the pattern in both of her previous marriages and was present in her relationship now.

Connecting with the root of why her relationships always seemed so volatile and doomed to fail was a huge moment for Jenny. She was able to see that when she gets upset about something that is happening in her relationship, it not only upsets her adult self but also, at times, will trigger the presence of that little girl, open up the pain from those wounds, and bring up the little girl's unresolved feelings from the past. It's not just Jenny, the adult, who is experiencing the heartache; it is also affecting the little girl within her. That is the very reason she is fleeing. She can't bear the possibility of being abandoned again like she was by her father. So when things seem to be headed in a negative direction, she quickly escapes so she can be the one leaving instead of her boyfriend.

In the following weeks, Jenny connected with the little girl who was abandoned and began to strengthen her connection and relationship with her. She affirmed for this little girl that she was going to take care of her now and she would never again leave her. Jenny specifically needed to reassure her little girl that she was here to help her now, because along with her father, at some point Jenny abandoned this little girl, too. This is often what happens. Someone abandons us and then we abandon ourselves as well. Or someone humiliates us and then we become the one who takes on that abusive behavior and continues the humiliation, either by humiliating others or ourselves.

As Jenny began to comfort this little girl and assure her that she would take care of her regardless of what was happening in her life or her relationship, she naturally became more able to stay and work through the issues in her relationship, instead of allowing herself to act on the impulse to flee and end the relationship. Although it took her forty years, Jenny was finally free from the limits that pivotal moment in her childhood created.

Maybe you can relate to being disconnected from that little girl or boy and not giving him or her enough attention. Maybe you've tried to distance yourself from the feelings that child felt back then or the desires this child still has now. Or maybe you have begun to treat yourself and your inner child negatively, taking on the critical behavior you received from a parent or sibling. Whatever you are feeling, reconnecting with this child will help this little girl or boy heal the unresolved feelings and experiences that he or she didn't know how to work through so you can grow, move past them, and create new experiences.

MY SPOTLIGHT

A Way Out of My Reality

When I was younger, I remember feeling like there was something different about me. I felt a huge disconnect between how I felt on the inside and the reality of my life on the outside. It wasn't anything anyone could see, but I just felt different inside than the way I showed up in life. It was as if there were two separate worlds: the way I acted in my so-called "real" life and then what was really happening within me. In my inner world, I felt like everything was possible—like I had this peaceful connection to something greater than me.

Yet, at the same time, I was aware that the things that were going on outside of me seemed to threaten that connection and peaceful feeling at every turn. I would watch the world and the events going on around me with confusion and disbelief, because what was happening inside of me did not correlate to what I was experiencing in the world and seeing around me. Many of the experiences in my outer world were loud and unbearable. And I didn't feel like I had the skills to cope with or make sense of them.

Although I never shared this with anyone as a child, now after all these years, I know what was happening within me. I was simply *connected*—deeply connected—to myself. I was extremely aware of my inner world and the deep connection I had with who I genuinely was at my core. Unfortunately, as the years passed, I lost this profound connection with myself as I struggled to make sense of and deal with the traumatic experiences I encountered.

Most of the time in my "real" life, I was just pretending that everything was okay and trying to ignore the blatant dysfunction that existed at the heart of my family life. I felt ashamed to share what was happening and, worse, I felt like I had to hide the truth. As I observed other kids' lives, I didn't see them experiencing the same things I was, so I thought there was something very wrong with us and with me, in particular. I also somehow took on the massive burden of being overly responsible for everything and everyone else. Inexplicably, I felt responsible for things I didn't have control of.

As a family, we were required to attend a treatment program. They believed that it wasn't only the alcoholic who was sick and suffering but that the whole family needed help. I remember feeling so violated as I was told to sit in a room with a counselor and tell him how I felt. The first issue I had with him was that he was a very large man and I was a little girl. I had absolutely nothing in common with him, and I felt extremely uncomfortable sharing my feelings with him.

During our first meeting, he said, "Share with me whatever you would share with your best friend—you know, everything you talk about." I remember in that moment feeling so angry that he was asking me to do that, and I immediately shut down. If I had been honest with him, I would have shouted at the top of my lungs, "What do you know about what it's like to watch somebody destroy themselves slowly while you sit back helpless, unable to do anything about it? And exactly how is me telling you how I *feel,* and everything I tell my best friend, going to help make any of it different?"

All I felt was anger and all I thought was, "Why would I share my most vulnerable thoughts with this complete stranger?" After all, I didn't want to be there and I simply wanted this nightmare to stop. Talking through my feelings with Joe, the abrasive, oversized counselor, wasn't going to help me get what I truly wanted. I just wanted it all to go away so I could go home and play with my friends.

Waiting For the Other Shoe to Drop

At some point, I decided that the treatment program was a farce, that it wasn't working, and I was going to have to take things into my own hands. So I began to watch the alcoholic like a hawk. I watched the moods, the fluctuation in vocal patterns, and any other indication that I could observe that would tell me whether we were headed for disaster or were in calm waters for the time being. That was one of the ways I became overly responsible at the young age of eleven. I became a keen observer of the alcoholic, and from that moment forward, everyone around me. That fear and obsession with others' behavior carried with me into adult life and kept me excessively focused on others' actions, behaviors, and motives instead of focusing on myself and my life. It created a feeling of insecurity within me and about most things around me, as I was always waiting "for the other shoe to drop."

For years, even when "good" things were happening, I was paranoid that something bad was just waiting around the corner. I also became extremely cautious, didn't trust anyone, and felt like I was on my own. One of the most detrimental and disturbing parts of all of this was that if you looked at my life from the outside, you would never have known any of this was going on. But as they say in recovery, "Our secrets make us sick." And this was a huge secret.

Also birthed from this secret, and the desperation to cover it all up, came my super-critical self that proclaimed that nothing I did was ever good enough. I felt that if I could just be better, get perfect grades, and achieve more and more, the drinking would stop and everything would be okay. But it wasn't okay, no matter how perfect a child I strived to be.

Maybe you can relate to feeling this way and trying to change who you are to please other people or control everything in your life. Maybe you too came from an alcoholic or dysfunctional family. Or perhaps you don't remember much dysfunction in your family life but were the youngest child and never felt like you could live up to your older sibling's talent or brilliance. As a result, you still live under the constant shadow of feeling like you have to prove yourself. Or maybe you were the firstborn and always felt like you had to take on more responsibility than your siblings. You've carried that resentment that you buried as a child for all these years and can now see that it still reappears at times. For example, when someone asks you to take on anything more than you feel you can handle, and you explode in frustration and anger.

Regardless of what you experienced as a child, taking this time to reconnect to yourself in this way will bring you to a place of wholeness and true peace. And the good news is that it's never too late. Reconnecting to our inner child gives us the gift of reconnection to our whole self. In addition, in this new relationship with ourselves, we have an extraordinary connection to our intuition and the answers we need in every moment of our lives. Reconnecting with that little girl or little boy within you will lead you to an amazing place of peace, safety, and comfort as well as a vast storehouse of answers, wisdom, and guidance.

Listen For That Little Voice

So how do you do this? You start by listening. You know that little voice in your head that sometimes proclaims:

- ◦ "It's *not* fair."
- ◦ "I want what she has."
- ◦ "I'm tired of feeling this way."
- ◦ "I can't take this anymore."

That's your inner child expressing herself. Yes, at times, he or she is screaming out obscenities at the top of his or her lungs and at other times timidly whispering for help.

Either way, listen for that voice. It may sometimes even be more like a feeling that comes over you than a voice you hear in your head. But that is the communication and expression of your inner child— the inner child who is observing the circumstances of your adult life and stomping her feet, proclaiming that she isn't getting what she needs, and wanting you to do something about it. Most important, this child wants you to hear her and change what is happening and what she is experiencing.

Often, as adults, we feel that we need to squelch this voice or quiet it in some way. But the converse is true. Remember how Jenny tried to quiet her little girl's voice by toughing it out and not acknowledging this little girl's feelings? Once she realized she was doing this and began to listen to her inner child, she was able to take control of what was occurring in her relationship. This voice of our inner child will guide us to the places where we need to focus our attention to make the changes we desire. Remember, our Inner Child is neither good nor bad, she just feels the way she feels based on our past experiences. And by listening to and honoring her feelings, you will be creating a powerful bond with this child. The renewed connection that you will have with this little girl or boy is essential to both your healing and being at peace with who you are. It is so worth you taking this time to connect, listen, and allow her to express her needs and feelings.

MY SPOTLIGHT

The Little Girl Left Behind

Here is what the voice of my little girl sounded like one casual Saturday morning.

Last December, I took my eight-year-old daughter to a new gymnasium to begin gymnastics. As I watched her for the first fifteen minutes, jumping about and freely moving her body, I began to feel tears welling up in my eyes. I turned my gaze a bit and also began watching the other girls do flip-flops and backflips and immediately began reminiscing about the days when I was a little girl on that floor bouncing about freely. Gymnastics had been a huge part of my upbringing, and I spent many hours sitting in front of the TV watching the Olympics, studying the gymnasts' every move and rehearsing in my mind what I was going to try at my gymnastics practice all week long. I was devoted to the sport. I absolutely loved it. And all these years later, the reconnection with this little girl and how she felt brought back some amazing memories as well as some sadness and grief. Why would it bring up so much sadness? Because I'm not physically that little girl who can do flip-flops and backflips and bounce about like that anymore.

Things change and we grow up into our adult selves. But I recognized, as I was feeling that grief and sadness, that I had a choice. I could just be sad or I could use it to grow and expand my life. As I chose the latter, I realized that I was missing something in my adult life. I was missing that feeling of jumping around and feeling agile and free in my body in that way. And although I can't now do what I could physically do at the age of fourteen, the little girl within me was crying out for more physical expression and movement in her body. It was this reconnection to my inner child that day that helped me realize this.

So that night I went home with my daughter and we did cartwheels and handstands in the living room. We played with wild abandon and moved freely in our bodies until the little girl within me was feeling alive and free again. Our reconnection to our inner child can be that simple.

EXERCISE

Your Turn: Taking Time to Listen

So how do you actually *listen* to and hear this child? You can connect with your inner child in many different ways. I will share a few of these techniques with you, and your job is to trust yourself and pick which one most resonates with you and your style. Choose from any of these methods below to connect with your inner child or create and design your own:

1. **Take out a picture of yourself as a child and look at this picture for a few minutes.** Really study yourself and where you were when that picture was taken. Notice if any feelings surface for you about who you were and what you felt back then.

    For example, "I loved this school picture of me. I was about eight years old and was wearing a red leotard against a blue background. Yes, for whatever reason, I wore my leotard to school picture day. I could see from looking at this picture how proud I was of who I was at that time in my life. It makes me smile to go back to that time."

Or, "I hated this time in my life. I was fifteen and lost. I remember that plaid shirt and how often I wore it. As I look at this picture and gaze into her eyes, I feel sorry for that awkward teenager who didn't have much support and was desperately seeking help."

2. **Close your eyes and return to a fond memory of you as a child.** Remember what you felt like, what life was like for you, and what made you most happy or at peace.

    For example, "I remember playing in my sandbox for hours. What I loved most about it was the solitude. I loved playing by myself and getting lost in what I was doing. It felt so peaceful and safe."

3. **Check in with your Inner Child whenever something upsetting or unsettling happens.** For example, if you have an argument with someone or if you get that feeling in your gut where you just don't feel good about what was said or done, take time to check in. Instead of hashing it out with the other person, close your eyes and sit with this little girl and just see how she feels. This will deepen your connection with her over time.

4. **Schedule a time in your calendar every day for the next seven days.** Close your eyes and visualize or emotionally connect with the little girl or boy within you. Ask this child, "How do you feel?, What do you need?, Do I listen to you enough?, How can I be more attentive to your needs and desires?" and "What was your desire for our life back when you were a child? How do you feel we are doing with fulfilling that? What is one thing you most desire that we could add into our life right now?" For example, alone time, down time, something special just for you, letting go of everyone else's needs and tending to your own, or a specific hobby or project.

You will begin to deeply connect with this little child by both listening to what she is experiencing and hearing what she needs. As you truly "hear" the needs of your inner child, you will begin to understand who she is and will be able to reconnect with her in a profound and impactful way. In addition, you will learn from her what you may need to do to help her embrace and move past what is currently going on in your life.

After you have taken time to listen to her needs and desires, you will want to move on to the next step in deepening your connection with this little child, which is to communicate your wisdom as an adult with her. One of the most important things for you to communicate with your inner child is that she is not re-experiencing what she did as a child.

Memorize and repeat this to yourself: *You are not re-experiencing what you did as a child.*

Depending on what you are currently experiencing in your life, it may be important to repeat this often to your inner child. *You are not re-experiencing the same thing you experienced as a child.* To your inner child, no matter how different the circumstances are, if a situation brings up a familiar emotion, it might feel the same. However, as we will explore now, it is very different. For example, your boyfriend, fiancé, or stepmother's behavior might remind you of the way your parent or sibling treated you as a child or could feel similar to something you experienced with a stepparent or a friend. But your inner child is not re-experiencing it the same way because you are no longer eight years old and you aren't powerless.

You are no longer that child, even though he or she is within you. You are an adult and you have a lot more resources. You have reason, logic, and can understand what's happening in a more profound way. You have the ability to get support for yourself and this child. You are not powerless like you may have felt when you were eight or ten or twelve. And that is what is most important to communicate with this child, especially when she is feeling upset or an experience is triggering some emotional response. Very simply communicate, "This is not the same." And most important, "I am here to help you now." This communication and awareness alone can bring you a lot of peace.

For example, when you are experiencing something difficult in your life and that little girl is feeling frustrated, upset, or angry, connecting with her and letting her know that you are going to take care of her will help her move to the passenger's seat and allow you, as the adult, to be in control. By doing this, she will feel more loved and cared for. And you, as the adult, will begin to feel more love and respect for yourself.

If you haven't done so yet, I invite you to reach into that box that may be tucked away somewhere in your closet and take out a picture of yourself as a child. You may be able to identify more deeply with this child if you can see a picture of that little girl or boy, as we travel this journey of reconnection. Go grab that picture right now and when you come back, we will begin to explore the language of our inner child. It is a powerful way to get to know yourself and this little child within you more intimately.

Our Inner Child's Language Is *Simplicity*

The language of our inner child is simplicity. Mostly what the little girl or little boy needs and wants at all times is love, compassion, safety, comfort, and security. Generously sprinkling in some joy, play, laughter, and fun is also essential. Now is a great time to begin to take stock of what you are bringing to this little girl or little boy in your life right now. Do you have these components at play in your day-to-day activities? Do you feel love or compassion toward yourself and your inner child? Do you bring that to yourself in times of struggle, challenge, or fear? Or is your current language of love with this little child being tough, pushing her along, and forcing her to comply with the demands of your adult life? Bringing awareness to our day-to-day interaction with our inner child is one way we can begin to bridge the gap between becoming serious, focused, and over-productive adults and re-integrating this little child into our life. When we become more connected to our inner child, we will find that the simplest of things become joyful again.

Use the exercise below to deepen this re-connection. And in the next chapter, you will discover how your inner child is being affected by your relationships and will learn what you can do to bring more of what you desire into each one of them.

Bite-Size Exercise

❖ ❖ ❖

Imagine that you could reconnect to some of the things that you've given up along the way, as you've grown from this little child to an adult. Maybe you wish that you were more playful or you could bring back some innocence, wonder, or curiosity to your life. You can. Let's do this now.

Go back to that picture of you as a child and look through the eyes of this little girl or boy. Think of the things that you most enjoyed when you were that age. What was it that really lit you up? Did you enjoy a simple 30 minutes in your sandbox in the backyard? Or riding your bike with the wind caressing your cheeks? Did you love music, lose yourself painting or sing wherever you went? These are all clues as to things that you can bring back into your life to nurture and support reconnection with your inner child. It doesn't need to have any other purpose than to fill you and your little girl or boy up.

Reconnecting doesn't have to be complicated. It is actually a very natural and simple process when we are aware of what's happening within us. My little girl has these adorable pigtails, and sometimes she is super bouncy and happy.

Other times when I connect with her, she's sullen and with-drawn. Her moods fluctuate depending on what's going on within me as well as what's happening in my life. But my heart always softens when I connect with her. I remember what it was like to feel that small, young, and innocent. I remember the world being a really big place and feeling really tiny in comparison. Sometimes I connect with this little girl on a daily basis if I'm going through something difficult and other times my connection with her is still present even though I'm not specifically closing my eyes and connecting with how she feels. Your journey to connection with your inner child will be unique to you. But whatever your journey is, it will deepen your sense of self and bring you immense peace.

Use the exercise below to deepen this re-connection. And in the next chapter, we will explore in more detail how your inner child is being affected by your relationships and what you can do to bring more of what you desire into each one of them.

Want More? Listen as I guide you through the exercise below on audio. Find the "Inner Child Connection" audio at www.dianealtomare.com/InnerChild

The Inner Child Connection Process

1. Imagine as you breathe into your heart that you could deeply connect with yourself and your breath. Just watch your breath and notice that with your focus and attention on your breath, you can gently move your breath two inches behind your navel to ground your breath in your abdomen.

Grounding your breath helps you to get into deeper connection with yourself.

2. On your next breath, bring to mind something about a relationship or experience in your life that you are not at peace with. Maybe it's an argument you just had or maybe it's something that is reoccurring in your life that you can't seem to change. Or maybe it's just the way you feel in general. Connect with the one thing you're most not at peace with and write it down.

3. Imagine that you could see this relationship or experience as it is right now. With your eyes closed, notice your interaction or how you are showing up in this experience. Without judgment, allow yourself to observe the circumstance and how you feel about it. Imagine being able to view it outside yourself as you become the observer of it. Jot down some notes. What does it look like? Maybe you feel out of control or you can't express what you want or need. Maybe you feel bad about what happened or unable to create what you want.

4. In a moment, we are going to look at this experience or situation, through the eyes of your Inner Child. Take a deep breath and imagine now sitting across from you is a version of you as a little girl. Notice what she looks like. Maybe she has pigtails and a cute dress and maybe she's happy to see you. Or maybe she feels beaten down, her head is hanging, and she is slouching over. Just notice what she looks like and how she feels.

5. On your next breath, ask this little child what it feels like to be in the current situation or experience that you are in. Does she feel safe, loved, and protected? If not, how does she feel? Maybe she feels scared, angry, or lost. Write down

whatever you are hearing or whatever you are feeling, as a result of what she is sharing.

6. Take another deep breath and ask this little girl what she most needs. What does she most need from you? If this experience or situation remains the same for the next few weeks, months, or years, what does she need from you? Maybe she needs love or protection. Or maybe she needs you to give her the benefit of the doubt. To stop blaming her or beating her up for how she feels. Maybe she needs support outside of you. Someone else who can help you see things through a different perspective. Ask her, "What do you need from me? How can I support you?"

7. Take a deep inhale and ask her what this experience, situation, or relationship reminds her of from her past? Maybe you watched your parents fight when you were young and that insecurity is surfacing now. Maybe it's the way that your mom dismissed you and now your significant other is doing the same. Take a deep breath and ask your inner child if this is a familiar experience or feeling she's having. And what about it feels familiar. Write down anything that she is sharing with you.

8. Take a deep breath and ask her, "What is one thing I can do this week to give you more of what you just requested? What is one action I could take or one thing I could do to reassure you, to love you, to have compassion for you, to take care of you, regardless of what is happening?" Maybe she needs you to be kinder to her and say nicer things to her. Maybe she needs you to get a picture of her and hang it up on the wall so that you remember that she is also being affected by what is happening in your life. Maybe she needs

you to journal about all the issues that are upsetting her or that are coming up for her in this situation. Maybe she needs you to get support or guidance.

Take a deep breath and ask her, "What is one thing that I can do this week to let you know that I'm listening to you and I'm here to support you?" If you're not receiving any guidance or messages, simply write down that you will connect with her again at least once or twice this week—that you will check in with her and see how she is doing.

9. Take another deep breath, look in her eyes, and take some time right now to communicate with her that you are here for her now. Make sure to tell her that you're going to develop a deeper relationship with her so that you can hear what she needs and she can express herself more often. Let her know that you will be there for her no matter what happens in your experience or relationship. You are here to love her, protect her, and keep her safe. And remind her that what is taking place right now in this experience, relationship, or situation is not the same as what occurred in the past. This is because you have so much more ability, intellect, understanding, wisdom, and resources than you did when you were a little child. Take some time to communicate that with your inner child. Write down any notes and make sure to put the action she's requested of you in your calendar.

Target What's Being Emotionally Triggered

Imagine sitting on a remote island with no one to talk to, no one to laugh with, and no one to hold your hand when you were scared. Without relationships, we would be alone and our days and nights would lack meaning. Certainly, our lives would be dramatically different. Think back to the past seven days of your life and notice how much time you spent interacting with other people. Relationships are a profound part of our daily experiences, and connecting to other people is almost as important as the oxygen we breathe. It is absolutely necessary for our basic survival and critical to the fulfillment of our purpose. Yet, for many of us, relationships aren't easy and are an area of our life where we continually struggle.

Take some time to reflect on the past six months of your life, and notice whether there was a challenge, struggle, minor issue, or a huge difficulty in any one of your relationships. As you reflect, you may find that you spent hours pining over this relationship, talking about what someone did or didn't do, trying to figure out the other person, or attempting to pinpoint what you did wrong. For so many of us, relationships often run our lives and determine whether we feel at peace or in turmoil. In this step you will discover how to create more of what you most want in your relationships—maybe love, connection, or a place where you feel safe, heard, and accepted. You will also learn how you can be at peace with yourself even when things are rocky or aren't going well in your relationships. The focus will be specifically on your significant or romantic relationship; however, you can use this wisdom for any relationship in your life.

Our Relationship Triggers

I'm single, in a committed relationship, married, divorced, separated, or widowed. A huge part of how we identify ourselves is by our relationship status. We make many judgments about who we are as a result of this identity, and this one area of our life has a heavy impact on how we experience our daily life. It determines minor things, such as a table for two or just one, whether we have a shoe-in date for Saturday night, or if someone is awaiting us when we arrive home from the airport to major things, such as who we choose to have children with or share our most intimate experiences with.

Many of us place a huge emphasis on our romantic relationships. Yet, as important as we may feel it is to have a significant other, we can't deny the fact that it comes with many challenges and, almost always, adds complexity to our life. At times, the other person brings a whole new layer of "issues" into our day-to-day experience. In difficult times, relationships can feel like a roller coaster that we don't quite know how to stop. Even in the healthiest of relationships, we still have problems to work through and differences to overcome. Everyone experiences challenges in their relationship at some point, and most of us have experienced that one huge conflict that seems to occur over and over again without much resolution.

MY SPOTLIGHT

From Broken to Happily Ever After

Between my twenties and thirties, I had a string of broken relationships. Relationships were something I struggled with deeply. I used to believe I just wasn't that good at them. Most of the time, being in a relationship just felt hard and un-natural to me.

Although I am now grateful to be married to an amazing man, I never dreamed about having a spectacular wedding or being married as a little girl. In all honesty, it always looked like a really bad idea to me. I didn't see many people in relationships who appeared "happy" or even content. In fact, it seemed to be a really excruciating experience for some of the couples I observed, and at the least, an unfulfilling experience for the others. But nonetheless, the drive to "be in a relationship" with a significant other is a universal pull that even I couldn't resist. It's just natural for us to want to share our lives with someone. And in my experience, it's a beautiful and amazing experience as long as we know how to maintain a healthy sense of self as a part of our "coupling."

But the concept of "falling in love" and "happily ever after" can be quite misleading if you aren't clear from the get-go about all that comes with that relationship. This very relationship that some of us have searched the ends of the earth for, will at times break you down, shake you to the core, stir things up, and have you questioning who you truly are.

So how do you find peace with a significant part of your life that will at times threaten to break you? First and foremost, you learn how to be at peace with who you are. You learn how to stop basing your worth and how you feel about yourself on what the condition of your relationship is in any moment. You learn what specifically this relationship is triggering or bringing up from the past. And, most importantly, you learn how to use this very relationship for a monumental purpose—your life's purpose—to grow and evolve into the person you are meant to be. The beautiful end result of all this growth and effort is a harmonious relationship that will empower you instead of break you and bring richness to your life instead of draining you of your energy.

Although this may not seem easy and may even appear to be a bit lofty and impractical for those of you who are seriously affected by your relationships, it is absolutely available to each and every one of us. And one of the most exciting parts of arriving at this place is that even when our relationships aren't perfect, or when things are happening that are hurtful or upsetting, you will know at a very deep level that you are okay.

Nonetheless, maybe right now, this doesn't seem possible to you in your relationship. Maybe you are so entrenched in the chaos or drama of your relationship that you don't know how to step back long enough to pay attention to how you are being emotionally triggered. Maybe you are too consumed with constantly thinking about the terrible things that were said, how badly you feel, or how you reacted to a particular situation. Maybe there's a feeling of desperation or a feeling of wanting things to be different so badly that you are at the end of your rope and don't know what to do other than give up or end the relationship. More times than not, that's what happens when we hit a place of conflict that we don't know how to resolve. We either end those relationships, cause chaos in them, or worse, we stay in the relationship and allow it to continue as it is without requiring anything different or doing what we need to do to make the changes we desire.

The Hope of Harmony

Regardless of how you are feeling about your relationship right now, you now have the tools to begin moving through whatever you are struggling with in this relationship and make the changes you desire. By using the exercises and techniques in this book, you will be so connected to who you are and what you are doing in your life, that you will be okay with you, regardless of what the other person in your life may be feeling or experiencing.

In this new place, you will be able to have compassion for your partner's experience and struggles without intertwining yourself in the chaos or the resolution of it. Whatever struggles or issues the relationship is bringing up for both of you is your "individual stuff" to look at, embrace, and make peace with before bringing it to each other's attention. In this moment and through this new perspective, you have the opportunity to see all of your "relationship problems" as solely "your problem, trigger, or issue" for now. Because when you step back and give yourself this time to first explore your part in the relationship and how you are being triggered by what is happening, you will be able to come to the relationship with wisdom and solutions instead of pointing your finger and starting a battle that can never be won.

CLIENT SPOTLIGHT

Marcus—Marriage Wreaks Havoc with Self-Esteem

Marcus, a forty-seven-year-old successful real estate professional, was in a marriage that was destroying his self-esteem. He felt lost and didn't understand why he felt so badly about himself. During our coaching session, I asked him to share with me what was happening in his home life and how he felt about his relationship with his wife.

"Most of the time," Marcus said, "I feel like I just don't measure up. Like I can't give her what she needs, and although I try really hard to please her, it never seems to work." He continued, "She's an amazing woman, so talented, hard-working, independent, and for the most part, she doesn't really need me."

I knew that the dynamic he and his wife had created had to be triggering something from his past, so I asked Marcus to tell me about his childhood.

Marcus proceeded to share that his mom died when he was six years old and his sister, who was thirteen at the time, pretty much took over. She became a mother figure to Marcus and he described her as often being mean and brash. He loved his sister and always gave her the benefit of the doubt because losing their mother was so tough on both of them. I asked him to describe their relationship.

"She was edgy and rigid, and sometimes she would play games with me and tie me up in the closet and leave me there for what felt like hours. I never said anything to my dad, as he was depressed most of the time and I felt like my sister was the only one I had. So I just tried to make her happy and do better, in the hopes that she wouldn't get angry or get into one of her moods."

Marcus was transferring his fear of his sister being a tyrant to his marriage, where he now feared his wife's demands, condescending tone, and unhappiness. His need to continually please his wife regardless of how she was treating him was the result of a little boy that just wanted love at all costs. Marcus had lost his voice thirty years ago in that closet and it was time for him to regain it.

Before Marcus would be able to speak up in his marriage, he had to reclaim the power he gave away to his sister. In addition, it was important for Marcus to let that little boy know that he didn't need the love and adoration of his wife in the same way he needed the love of a mother figure when he was that young impressionable child. While he, of course, desired a strong bond with his wife, he didn't need it in the desperate way he needed that bond when he was a little boy. This was an essential realization for Marcus to discover.

Marcus was able to see through reconnecting with this little boy how and why he had relinquished his power. This was a huge step for him to admit, as he always felt like he was defying his sister whenever he said something that challenged how she had raised him. He always came to her defense declaring that "she did the best she could and was just trying to cope with our mother's abrupt death." While this was absolutely true, it was important for him to acknowledge how he had given up his voice and put aside his needs to obtain love.

For thirty days after our session, Marcus's assignment was to close his eyes and communicate with this little boy and ask him how he was feeling and if there was anything he needed to communicate or express.

After just a few days of doing this "Inner Child Connection" process, Marcus was starting to realize how much he truly had to say and how often he had been biting his tongue. By the end of his assignment, Marcus was getting pretty good at being able to communicate his needs and feelings with his wife and felt much more at peace with their relationship dynamic. For the first time, in as long as he could remember, he began to communicate what he needed. Even the simplest things, such as where he wanted to go for dinner and what activities he wanted to do with their friends who were coming into town the following month, were voiced. And then also, in the moments when his wife was unhappy or condescending, he was able to communicate how he felt and not shut down. This was huge progress for Marcus and he was elated as he felt like an equal participant in his marriage for the first time.

Insight About Marcus

For Marcus, his feelings of being submissive to his sister were reappearing in his marriage in the moments when his wife was demanding and condescending. His work was to continue to take care of the little boy within who shut down in those moments and give him permission to speak up. By regaining this voice, Marcus was able to begin to communicate his needs and what was most important to him to his wife. He was now able to be present in his marriage as a confident adult and not an insecure little boy.

The Root of It All

So why are relationships so challenging, and what is the root of all of this struggle? The dissatisfaction and disharmony in all of our relationships stems from a place of disconnection, first from ourselves and then from the other person. The difficulty in our relationships occurs when we make someone else responsible for our choice to disconnect from ourselves. Even though this choice may have been unconsciously made, disconnecting and not honoring our truth, our needs, and our contribution to the relationship opens us up to a host of potential problems.

One of the ways we avoid this inner reflection and connection to ourselves is by blaming each other. This often starts an endless cycle of disconnection, because when we make the other person responsible for how we feel and what is going on within us as a result of the relationship, we are once again feeding the disconnection that often started years earlier.

The opportunity that you have in this moment is to completely shift the way you think about your relationship as well as yourself. However, before we do that, we have to demystify a fairytale that may be tough for some of us to let go of. . . .

There is no white knight on horseback coming to save you, make everything okay, or fulfill your dreams. And despite that most famous line declared by Jerry Maguire, the other person is not here to "complete you," or even to make you happy.

As Harville Hendrix shares in *Getting the Love You Want,* "Our unconscious mind chose our partner for the purpose of healing childhood wounds." Our significant other is really here to show us who we are, where we are in our evolution, and guide us to the places where we need to heal and reconnect to ourselves. The only true "completion" that we have the opportunity to experience from our relationships is embracing all of who we are and being at peace with every single part of ourselves.

Although this is an individual journey, the beauty of this journey is that once you feel and experience that reconnection to yourself, you will be able to meet your significant other in a space of contribution instead of neediness, a place of overflow instead of lack, and a space of abundance instead of depletion. And the irony is that you will feel more connected to them than ever before. From this new place of connection, you will be able to contribute who you are, share your uniqueness and brilliance with your partner and play in the magnificent exchange of their gifts to you as well.

However, despite how significantly relationships can help us evolve and become the best version of ourselves, there is a part of us that knows the other side of relationship bliss. There is a part of us that knows that relationships can be downright scary at times.

We all know that buried deep within even the most precious of relationships lies the potential for loss. And the fear of that loss is often what begins to guide our actions and hold us back from being fully committed and deeply connected to our significant other. Every human being experiences heartbreak at some point in his or her life. Whether it was your parents' divorce in childhood, the breakup of your first true love, or a rift in a relationship with a sibling as you grew up, we have all been impacted by the loss of love or loss of connection that a relationship once brought. The feelings that we experience as a result of that loss, breakup, or divorce can often be overwhelming and difficult to accept. Often the heartbreak can "live on," especially if we didn't or weren't able to focus on consciously healing after the dissolution of the relationship.

If you tried to avoid, deny, or push away how you were truly feeling at the time, you are left with the residue of those unresolved emotions or experiences within you. If you experienced the pain of your parents' divorce when you were a child, you may not have had the support or ability to understand how you were feeling in order to process all of your emotions. As a result of your inability to "make sense" of the heartache, you may never have recovered fully from those experiences. You could now be experiencing the fallout of that heartbreak and the transferring of your fears, pain, or resentment from your past into your current relationships. All that pain, resentment, and fear is part of the contents in your transference box and is being transferred in some way from your past into your current experiences. Remember, by definition, transference is the continuation of our past way of being in an earlier relationship into a current one.

If we want to create something new in our relationships, we must look at these past feelings and experiences and allow them to guide us to the places we need to heal. To our detriment, however, we often avoid dealing with what our current relationship is dredging up from the past. We may not be conscious of how it's mirroring a relation-ship we've previously had. Instead we find ourselves denying our part in what's not working and focusing on the other person's behav-ior. Even if the other person is behaving "negatively," there is always something essential for us to learn from our experience with them. When we fail to bring this conscious awareness to ourselves and our relationships, we risk repeating the patterns of our past or reacting from a place of fear. From this place, healing isn't possible and we often create more chaos for ourselves than we intended.

Letting Go of Right and Wrong

Although using the challenges in our relationships to heal is an essen-tial component of our growth, it can be difficult to look at our part, which is often the reason we may pay more attention to our part-ner's actions instead of our own. Rather than allowing ourselves to explore how we are a part of creating the relationship, we may often find it easier to make the relationship struggles the other person's fault. Frequently, the reason the relationship isn't working is because each person is blaming the other person. This "I'm right and you're wrong" dynamic in any relationship sets up the relationship to have a winner and a loser. In this way of being in a relationship, each person is focused on criticizing the other person instead of spend-ing the time, focus, and energy on going deeper into how they may be unconsciously recreating their past relationships. Each person is declaring to the other, "If you would just change, everything would be okay."

Maybe you've experienced this in your relationships or witnessed it in someone else's. Unfortunately, when we are focused on someone else's behavior instead of our own, there is little room for growth and not much actually changes.

So how do you make lasting changes and actually heal your rela-tionship? Often you will find that there is a cycle of behavior or a pattern of interaction that continues repeatedly and neither you nor your partner can figure out how to do anything differently. If you are experiencing this pattern, it is time to look at how you may be transferring feelings from the past. Most moments in your relationship that leave you feeling like there is no resolution, or leave you feeling frustrated, hopeless, or resigned, are gifts waiting to be uncovered. Those moments are a great indicator that there may be some way you are showing up in your relationship that mirrors or triggers an experience you had with a parent or sibling in childhood.

You may at times feel as if there is no other way to react or respond when your partner is acting a certain way. But there is always an alternative way of being in a relationship and many different options available to us, even if we can't see them yet. Doing the work to heal ourselves first allows us to open up to new ways of connecting and responding to our partner as well as deepens our understanding of the way we show up in all of our relationships.

CLIENT SPOTLIGHT

Rebecca—Accepting His Wavering Love

Rebecca, a thirty-seven-year-old mother of two young children, was really struggling in her marriage. Most of the other areas of her life were going pretty well, but she spent a great deal of time being upset with her husband and trying to get him to change. Her biggest complaint about her husband was that he would often disconnect from her and "take away the love he gave." During our first phone coaching session, she described her husband as loving, charming, and attentive some of the time. But the problem she had was that he was only that way sometimes. At other times he would completely disconnect from her and withdraw his love, affection, and adoration. In those moments, she would feel crushed—as if the wind was being knocked out of her and she couldn't breathe.

Now, of course, no one likes feeling disconnected with his or her spouse. But Rebecca's reaction seemed out of proportion to what her husband was doing, which was sometimes being wrapped up in work, not making time for her, or being more focused on the kids than their relationship. It's possible that he could have been a more attentive husband; however, Rebecca's reaction of devastation didn't match what was actually happening.

As we explored her feelings further, Rebecca began to make a connection to feelings she felt about her dad when she was younger. Her dad was an alcoholic, and throughout her childhood, he was often asked to leave the house or leave parties because of his drinking. She remembered feeling this insecurity and immediate disconnection when he would leave and she didn't know where he was.

Before Rebecca could feel better about her relationship with her husband, she had to acknowledge that the feelings she had when she felt disconnected from her husband were related to the experience and relationship she had with her dad when she was a child. It was also important for her to let that little girl know that she was now an adult and could take care of herself in a new way. She no longer needed her dad or her husband to be present in order for her to feel safe or okay. That was an important step in Rebecca's healing process.

Rebecca was able to then use this pain to see how she was abandoning herself and not taking care of herself in the way she needed to. She was able to see how much she was relying on the adoration and love of her husband to feel good about herself. As she began to understand why she was reacting so intensely to her husband disconnecting from her, she was able to more effectively comfort herself and that little girl within her in those moments. This realization was powerful for Rebecca, not only in her relationship, but in her life as a whole. She began to see how often she would put aside her own needs and desires to focus on trying to get her husband to change. Throughout the time we worked together, she regained her sense of self by refocusing her attention on her needs, desires, and what she wanted in her life. Instead of her intense focus on what was lacking in their relationship, she began to take amazing care of herself as well as bring things into her life that filled her up.

She had a charity that she was really passionate about that she decided to become an active participant in, and to this day, does amazing work with. She also re-engaged with one of her long-time friends and planned a weekly coffee date. Rebecca thoroughly enjoyed this special time with her dear friend, as she felt so loved, supported and filled up from their weekly chats and connection. All of this was possible once she specifically identified the root of her dis-satisfaction and pain.

By doing this inner reflection, she was able to reclaim her power, feel more confident, and allow her husband to be himself. In addition, because she now knew what was happening, she was able to ask her husband to re-connect with her when she felt that disconnec-tion, instead of going into the wounds of her little girl self. As a result, their relationship began to improve and she began to feel more inde-pendent and gain more self-love.

Insight About Rebecca

Could her husband have improved the way he treated her at times? Probably. But the power in doing this work is that you don't have to wait for someone else to change. You can look within to see how you are being triggered and can do the deep work to heal that wound, rather than poking and prodding at someone else's wound, which doesn't fix anything. Even if the problems in your relationship are more serious than Rebecca's, such as an unfaithful spouse or an alco-holic partner, your work is still to focus on how you are being affected and what from your past the situation is triggering. With this clarity and understanding, you will have more insight as to what your neces-sary and next steps will be in your relationship.

For Rebecca, her feelings of being abandoned and alone in her childhood were being transferred to her marriage in the moments when she felt her husband displaying similar behavior to that of her dad. Her work will be to continue to notice when she feels lonely and afraid like she did when she was a little girl and acknowledge her ability to make different choices as an adult. Instead of unconsciously going into the past fear and loneliness she experienced as a child, she can make a new choice from her adult self. She can choose to love herself in those moments when her husband disconnects from her, or she can choose to find connection and support from other people in her life during those times. When we are conscious of the real root of our behavior, we can make the changes necessary to take care of ourselves, even when we feel the feelings of the past arise.

Playing Out Our Wounds

As we have seen, even without recognizing it, we can easily play out our childhood wounds in our relationships. Our partner, spouse, or in-law triggers us in some way and we may trigger or affect that person as well. Then unconsciously or consciously, in order to "deal" with and actually deflect our feelings, we engage in a battle of pointing the finger away from ourselves and towards the other person. In that moment, we are simply showing up in our child self and the other person is showing up in their child self. We are replaying the unresolved experiences from our childhood and are acting out our wounds together. This inner child dueling inner child experience does not allow us to move beyond either the current issue or the past hurt. In this battle, we are simply placing our hurts and unresolved feelings onto the other person. We are making it the other person's fault that we feel the way we do or are being affected in a certain way. You may have experienced this in your relationship. It sounds something like this:

- "I hate the way you make me feel."
- "I can't deal with the way this relationship makes me feel."

○ "Your actions hurt me, you make me feel insecure, and when you stop doing that, I will be happy."

If we truly want to heal our own wounds, we must take back our projections and focus on how this relationship can help us grow. Once we do our own individual healing, we will be able to show up in the relationship in a new and more powerful way. We then won't be triggered as deeply by our relationship or will be able to recognize when we are negatively affected much more quickly.

The benefit of doing our own individual healing in our relationships is profound. The experience of the relationship becomes much more free, fun, and playful like it was at the beginning. In addition, when we aren't playing out "our unresolved pain" from our childhood or bringing our past into our relationships there is space to create something new. Being conscious of how people naturally "play out" their wounds in relationships gives us the foresight to notice when the other person in the relationship is playing out "their stuff." And, more important, it gives us the insight as to what is occurring so we don't engage in it when it does take place.

We are all affected by our relationships in some way. By being conscious of this, you can identify the situations where you are being triggered and work on whatever the situation is bringing up for you. The goal is to become more conscious of how and when this happens. You can then also see where you may be triggering someone else and allow them the space and freedom to do their own healing work. It is a much more conscious way of being in your relationships.

Once you begin to engage in your relationships in this new way, you have the opportunity to create deeper and more profound connections. From this new place of being, you may feel more able to share how the relationship is affecting you. Explaining that something from your past is triggering your reaction to a current situation can deepen your relationship. It can help the other person understand you in a more meaningful way. And they will often be grateful that you aren't placing your issues on them or blaming them for your feelings. When you share how this relationship is helping you grow, it may open up the space for them to see how they are being affected or triggered as well. They then may realize that they have their own work to do.

Cindy—Needy Divorced Girl In Love

Cindy, an executive assistant, was in her early fifties and had been divorced for about ten years. She had been in a new relationship with a man she truly adored for about three months before she started to feel some very familiar and uncomfortable feelings. She really enjoyed his company but was starting to feel "too needy" in her relationship with him. She thought about him a lot, wondered what he was up to and was always anticipating his call. She literally checked her phone ten times a day to see if he had called or texted. She loved the time they spent together but found that lately, she was calling him more often than he would call her and it just didn't feel good to her.

She had also begun to notice that when she reached out to him from this "needy" place, she often received the opposite reaction she desired. It seemed to turn him off in some way. She was contemplating breaking it off with him when we began working together, as she just wasn't getting the attention she needed. She expected the man she was dating to want to talk to her daily, and for some reason, he just didn't seem to want to do that. She said, "When I bring it up, he shuts down and won't talk about it and that upsets me even more."

During our first few phone sessions, Cindy shared details of the difficult relationship she had with her mom and how she felt about it. "My mom was cold and distant and didn't seem to be present most of the time when I truly needed her. I felt discounted by her a lot and she rarely knew much about what was going on in my life." She continued, "I guess I am sort of feeling the same way with my boyfriend.

He always seems to have so many things to do and a lot of them don't include me." Cindy was beginning to understand that there was a connection here—her boyfriend "rejecting her"when she needed him was an experience she had in the past with her mom. Cindy began to understand that this new relationship was triggering the wounds that had been present since she was a little girl.

As she began to see what her new relationship was uncovering for her and not blaming her boyfriend for shutting down when she confronted him, she could refocus her attention back to herself and honor the feelings of that little girl who felt rejected by her mom. This was a huge step for Cindy, as she had never really acknowledged how insecure she felt as a little girl around her mom. She shared how she always felt like she was in her mom's shadow and wasn't ever the center of attention. It was always about what her mom needed. Cindy felt like she was often just there to serve her mom.

She told me how she asked for new skates one year and remembered the look of total disgust on her mom's face, as she declared, "Don't make everything all about you Cindy." This was often her mother's response to whatever she asked for and little by little, Cindy began to shut down and not ask for much from her mom. She didn't realize the impact it had on her then and was still having on her now. As she worked on listening to the feelings of this little girl within, she started to feel more connected to herself and her own needs, instead of putting pressure on her brand new relationship to make her feel secure.

Insight About Cindy

Once Cindy could uncover the root of her insecurity, which was the disconnection she originally felt from her mom as a little girl, she began to understand why she was being triggered and what she needed to do. She realized it had nothing to do with her boyfriend's actions and was all being triggered from her past. In bringing consciousness to herself and what was waking up her "too needy" feeling, she felt more control over herself and her life.

She could now, from this new place of understanding and compassion for herself, take care of herself and understand why she felt "needy" at times. Instead of then transferring this neediness to her relationship, she would close her eyes and connect with the little girl within her and ask, "How can I take care of you?" And "How can I support you in feeling secure and loved?" Fortunately, because Cindy became aware of how she was re-creating her past, she was able to catch it before she destroyed her new relationship. And because she was conscious of the transference that was taking place, she was able to look at what was happening in her relationship as an opportunity to heal her past and create a different outcome.

As a result of working together, Cindy was able to regain her sense of self, become more connected to her needs and was less needy in her relationship. From this place, her relationship was thriving and surprisingly enough, her boyfriend started calling more often. She loved their new connection and loved the feeling of him caring for her in that way, although she had come to realize that she didn't "need" it the way she had before. She did, however, love their new way of interacting. This was the first time Cindy felt like she was in a healthy relationship.

Your Most Difficult Relationship

When you can understand another's pain, you can truly understand why they are the way they are. The key to being able to transform our relationships is not only to understand our own experience and journey but also to understand others' experiences. People are always operating from and responding to life from their own perspective and from the totality of their experiences. You can use your new understanding of transference to make peace with the most difficult relationship in your life by understanding the pain that person may be unconsciously transferring onto you and the relationship. By acknowledging what experience, issue, or trauma they are playing out with you, you will be able to understand them better. Once you can understand that you are simply triggering an unresolved hurt, incident, or emotion from their past, you can give yourself permission to not take it personally and disconnect from their pain. In other words, you can allow them to be as they are.

Where "I" Stop and "You" Begin

As Esther Hicks, author of *Getting into the Vortex* states, "If you do not take another's behavior personally, understanding it is their personal battle—in time, they will leave you out of it." So how do we stay out of it? How do we not take someone's behavior personally? We do this in two ways: first by learning the boundary lines between us and then with the practice of disconnection. Yes, this is a place where disconnection is helpful and is a powerful tool.

Although our boundary lines may not always be crystal clear, part of the journey to healing lies in understanding where we end and someone else begins. When we do our own inner healing work, we become intimately connected to our "stuff"—our issues, wounds, and challenges. By recognizing our own challenges and struggles, we can then choose to focus only on what we can change and allow others to do their own inner work and healing. We are not responsible for someone else's actions, behaviors, or the way they respond to something we are doing. The only person that we are responsible for is ourself. Identifying the boundary lines between us gives us clarity on the other person's issues as well as our own.

Once we have clarity on what we are being affected by and what we need to work through, we can allow the other person to work through their issues, not take them on, and not take their actions personally. Sometimes this can be hard to do in a relationship because we are so interconnected with each other. However, it's essential to make sure that you know when someone else's stuff is coming up so that you can let them take care of it on their own and not take it on.

So how do we that? How do we not take on someone else's baggage, feelings, or experiences? We learn and practice disconnecting.

Disconnection is a healthy practice and is the way we protect ourselves. By being able to disconnect from what someone else is going through, we allow ourselves the space to have our own experience and not become enmeshed with whatever they are experiencing.

So in the moment you see your partner angry, frustrated, or upset, for example, practice disconnecting or detaching yourself from their emotions and experience. For people who want to be empathetic, this may seem cold or selfish. However, we don't help others deal with their issues by taking on their pain; it truly does not assist them at all. You can actually be more supportive to someone when they are going through a difficult time by staying in your own energy and emotions and not going "there" with them. It's actually more of a burden on someone if you are adding your emotion to what they are already experiencing.

For those of us who are sensitive or emotional by nature, it is sometimes difficult to separate our emotions from someone else's. So when someone cries, for example, you might feel like crying or really feel their pain. For you, especially, it is important that you learn how to disconnect from someone else's feelings and stay connected to yourself. Connection to yourself is the way you guard yourself from taking on another's feelings, challenges, or issues. By practicing being connected to your own feelings, what's going on within you, and what you may need to do to take care of yourself in that moment, you will not become entangled in the other person's experience. You can instead bring something valuable to the relationship. By staying connected to ourselves in this way, we can create deeper connections with others, and from this place, our relationships can thrive.

Hope—The People-Pleaser's Need to Fix

Hope, a forty-five-year-old interior decorator was a fixer. She hated to see people unhappy, especially her husband. So whenever he had a problem, Hope would get involved in the issue, as if it were her own. She took on all of his problems and would spend countless hours counseling him and trying to figure out what would make him happy. She knew the specific look of discontent he would get on his face and when she saw that look, she knew she had a project in front of her. In those moments, she would literally feel his feelings, jump into the boxing ring with him, and spend hours finding a solution. Unfortunately, most of the time, the solutions she came up with didn't feel right to him. And he often didn't use the advice she had spent hours formulating. Hope always felt crushed and let down when he proceeded to handle the issue "his way."

During one of our phone sessions, Hope began to identify the reason that she would drop everything in her life and run to his rescue, even when he didn't ask for help. I shared with her that often we are over focused on someone else's life, because we are avoiding something in our own. I assured her that what she was most avoiding was the key to unlocking a new place of contentment and peace in her own life. I guided her to identify the core feeling she had about every area of her life. We started with her relationship to her body, as she had been battling weight issues for years. I asked her, "How do you feel about yourself and your body?" Hope said, "I feel like a failure, like I've let myself down and just don't have what it takes to stay disciplined and lose weight. I've pretty much given up."

Hope's assignment for the next seven days was to identify how she was feeling that specific day about herself and her body. As she began to journal about her feelings, she uncovered the different emotions that were present and took the time to connect with each emotion as it arose. As she did this inner exploration, she noticed a familiar pattern. There were many other times in the past when she diverted attention from herself and her problems and began to focus on someone else, as a way to avoid what was happening in her life.

Insight About Hope

Throughout the time we worked together, Hope learned that she was focusing on the "fixing of others" in an attempt to not deal with the struggles in her own life. It was a way that she created a fantasy world where she didn't have to face her own issues.

Hope's work was, of course, to reconnect to herself in the moments she felt pulled to "fix" someone else. She also started to work on staying connected to her feelings of love for her husband and the belief she had in him, knowing that he could figure out a solution for himself. From this place, she was able to bring him comfort and support instead of taking on his problems and creating dissension in their relationship. As a result of doing this, her husband felt much more love and support from her and their relationship became stronger. They began to take long walks again every night and just casually chat about their lives, like they used to love to do. It became easier for Hope to just listen to her husband's experiences without needing to fix his problems. She also began a new health regimen where she lost 30 pounds, was exercising three times a week and felt great about her health and body. By refocusing attention on herself and her life, Hope was able to make significant changes in both her relationship with her husband and with her weight loss goals.

In the next step, you will uncover the default emotion that is running your life and controlling your actions.

But first, use the following exercises to gain some freedom and clarity in your relationships.

Bite-Size Exercise

❖ ❖ ❖

Identify the relationship in your life that is the most challenging for you right now. Remind yourself over the next few days, as you interact with this person that you are learning a new way of being in relationship with yourself and others. And most importantly, that this relationship and experience will get better over time, as you continue to engage in your inner work.

Want More? Listen as I guide you through the "Relationship Healing" exercise on audio. Find the "Relationship Healing" audio at www.dianealtomare.com/relationshiphealing

EXERCISE

The Relationship Healing Process

1. Imagine as you breathe into your heart that you can deeply connect with yourself and your breath. Just watch your breath and notice that with your focus and attention on your breath, you can connect deeply to how you are currently feeling about yourself and your relationship.

2. Take a deep breath and allow yourself to connect to a conversation or situation in your relationship that you don't feel at peace with—something that feels unsettled or you don't feel good about.

3. Allow yourself to connect with the feelings that you are feeling about this relationship or situation. What does it feel like

to be connected to this person in this way? Notice whatever feelings are present. Just breathe into those feelings and notice where in your body they live.

4. Take a deep breath and allow yourself to see how you are most being triggered by this relationship or situation. How is this relationship causing you upset, dissatisfaction, or pain? Identify specifically what is causing you to feel upset and write it down.

5. On your next breath, allow yourself to notice what this is triggering or bringing up for you from your past. How is this similar to something you have experienced before? Notice the ways this feels familiar to you.

6. Take a deep breath and connect with what you most need to learn from this relationship. How is this relationship helping you to grow? Or what can you learn from this relationship?

7. Finally, ask yourself, "What action can I take this week to find peace within myself regardless of the state of this relationship? What is one thing I can do to nurture myself and acknowledge how I am growing as a result of this very relationship?" Maybe you can practice disconnecting from your partner's feelings or identifying how learning this lesson from this relationship will help you develop into more of who you are meant to be.

8. Trust whatever answer comes to you. Just breathe into whatever this new realization is creating within you. Maybe you feel a little more peace or clarity. Breathe into this and write down a few notes.

Remember to put your action step in your calendar so you can complete the action that came from this exercise.

Discover Your Default Emotion

You may have noticed, as you have been working through each of the previous steps that there is an emotion you tend to feel more predominantly than others. Maybe it's your anger. Perhaps it's frustration. Or maybe you frequently feel guilty or tend to feel negative about whatever is happening.

Your default emotion is most likely running your life.

One of my clients recently said, "I am now so aware of how limiting my default emotion is. It is like a room I keep running to that keeps me from facing what is bothering me. I'm now giving myself the permission to 'run' to a different room when I get 'frustrated or resigned' in reaction to things not going my way."

Identifying your default emotion is the next step to living from the inside out and creating something new in your life.

Identify Your Default Emotion

CLIENT SPOTLIGHT

Amanda—Feeling Powerless

Amanda, a forty-two-year-old fitness enthusiast and stay-at-home mom came to our session feeling both upset and resigned. She felt powerless over her life and specifically over her husband's actions during the past few weeks. He had a chronic problem with taking and abusing prescription pain pills, and although he was sometimes by himself when he took them, he was often with her or, worse, with their children. She shared how a few weeks ago, she came home from a social gathering to find him passed out on the couch, while the girls were in their bedroom doing their homework. I could hear the desperation in Amanda's voice, as she shared how fed up she was with his behavior and how hopeless she felt because she didn't know what to do about it. "He acts like someone else when he is drugged up; it's scary, like I don't even know him. He gets this jolly happy-go-lucky joker smile on his face and his personality just switches to that of an irresponsible teenager. I feel so alone, like I'm parenting the girls on my own."

As she began to share more details of what had happened the previous week, she continued to affirm how the situation was out of her control: "I've tried to talk to him many times; I've begged and pleaded with him to change his behavior but nothing is working. And I feel like there's nothing I can do." Amanda was holding steady to her interpretation of the experience and wasn't budging. I knew that she was covering up her true feelings about the situation and resorting to powerlessness because it kept her from having to deal with what she really felt. It was time to go deeper and connect with the real emotions underneath this default emotion of powerlessness.

Amanda had shared in our previous phone sessions that her dad wasn't present throughout most of her childhood. As a little girl, she felt like she didn't have any control over when and if he ever came back. She felt out of control and powerless because she didn't feel like she could do anything about how little her dad was a part of her life.

As we discussed the current situation with her husband, I asked Amanda to connect with the little girl within her that felt these same feelings of powerlessness that she was feeling now. She said she saw the little girl sitting in front of her but she wasn't doing or saying anything. Again, powerlessness. After several minutes of resistance in connecting with this little girl and her feelings, I asked Amanda to ask the little girl, "What did it feel like when your dad wasn't there for you? When he didn't show up for your events?"

She took a deep breath and blurted out, "I felt angry. I couldn't believe he would do that to me. I had so much rage inside of me that sometimes it just took over and I didn't know what to do. Then one day I just gave up wanting him to be there anymore. I quit being angry; it felt hopeless to feel anything at all."

Amanda was finally beginning to see what the little girl truly felt. Beneath the hopelessness and powerlessness, she felt rage and anger. She could now see she was feeling the same way about her husband's behavior, and she had been burying her true feelings just like she learned to do as a child. Amanda could now be honest with herself about what she *really* felt about her husband's drug abuse. She felt anger that he would resort to this and rage that he would put his children's lives at stake.

Her work after our session was to allow herself to feel the rage and anger whenever it was present. In addition, she took both emotions on a walk and allowed them to communicate with her. By asking the rage and anger, "What are you here to express to me or communicate with me?" she received the guidance of these emotions and was able to stand in powerful action to take care of herself and her children. Her rage and anger communicated, "Speak up. Communicate boundaries with your husband. The only voice your children have right now is yours."

Amanda heard this wisdom loud and clear and as a result, scheduled an appointment with a licensed professional and her husband for later that week. In this session, she was able to communicate her boundaries clearly and have the support of a licensed professional to affirm that it wasn't ok for him to be impaired in anyway when he was in charge of the kids. He agreed and also committed to future sessions with the counselor. After a few months of continuing with her individual phone sessions and more couples' sessions with the counselor, their marriage is stronger than ever and their kids are happy and safe. Although, her husband is still in recovery, they are feeling connected again and she has begun to trust him. She feels safe leaving the girls with him and no longer feels like she is the only parent in the house. They have also begun to go to the movies once a month for a date night and are enjoying long talks during Sunday morning coffee together again.

Insight About Amanda

In dealing with her husband's drug abuse, she had resorted to the powerless place she experienced as a little girl, even though she was a grown woman. In order to reclaim her power, she had to learn to identify when her default emotion was emerging and dig deeper to determine what was really going on underneath the surface. Her ability to communicate clear boundaries and set up the appointment with the counselor was a direct result of moving beyond her powerlessness.

For many of us, anger and rage are both uncomfortable emotions. But Amanda's unconscious choice to not deal with the feelings of rage and anger caused her to not be able to see what she needed to do to take responsibility for her life. She went to her default emotion of powerlessness because it had simply become her way of being. However, resigning to the state of being powerless was preventing her from connecting with her true needs and her desire to take care of herself and her children. It was holding her back from powerfully communicating with her husband and setting boundaries. Instead, in the energy of powerlessness, she suppressed her needs and thoughts and allowed him to do whatever he thought was best.

Your Default Emotion Is Running Your Life

Your default emotion is the emotion you go to often, even if it doesn't fit the situation or is an inappropriate response to the circumstance. It covers up some deeper emotion that you don't want to or don't know how to feel or acknowledge. Feeling powerless wasn't what Amanda *needed* to feel, and powerlessness wasn't the emotion that held the real message. It is always the emotions underneath our default emotion—the emotions that we are often avoiding—that will propel us forward into appropriate action. If you ignore them, you can't fully understand and address what's truly going on within you.

We all have a default emotion. It is an emotion that we got stuck on at some point in our life because we experienced the emotion too often or simply because we didn't know how to process it when it was arising. Maybe there was a lot of sadness in your past and you didn't know how to move through that sadness and process the experience. So sadness then becomes your default way of responding when a situation is difficult or upsetting to you. You are literally stuck in the sadness. Or maybe you felt a lot of anger as a child and you didn't know how to process the anger and move through all of it, so you became stuck in that emotion and it is now what you use to respond to most situations.

Our default emotion is an emotion that we tend to be more comfortable with, familiar with, or used to feeling. But if you don't get to the deeper emotions, you won't be able to address what's truly going on and make the changes you desire.

Avoidance Emotions

In order to start truly living from the inside out, we have to take a serious look at the emotion we find ourselves expressing most often. We can then identify the root of that emotion, why it has become a coping mechanism for us, and learn how to move beyond that emotion so that we can access the real emotion underneath it. By identifying and embracing the "true emotions" underneath the default emotion, you give yourself the gift of release. We will call the "true emotion" underneath the default emotion our "avoidance emotion." In other words, the emotions we are avoiding or can't seem to connect to. Let's take a closer look at how this works.

Melinda—Feeling Immense Sadness

Melinda, a forty-five-year-old executive was in desperate need to let go of the immense sadness she was feeling when she arrived at our session one afternoon. She had been feeling sad a lot lately and didn't know what to do to change it. The first thing I asked her was, "Is this a familiar emotion? Do you remember feeling sad at other times in your life?" She shared that she had felt sad most of her life, and then she began to share more about why. Her mom had been sick much of her life, and as a result her mom couldn't be there for Melinda in a way that Melinda really needed her to be. She remembered the other moms always being at school events and her mom being at home. She would often be picked up by someone else's mom to go to softball practice and her mom was rarely able to attend games.

As Melinda identified what happened and how that felt as a little girl, she began to feel grief and acknowledge how difficult it was for that little girl to grow up with a mom who was always sick. As Melinda continued to work through the grief, she saw other emotions underneath the sadness, including the one she was avoiding the most: anger.

As we went deeper, she also began to uncover her belief that life wasn't fair. She remembered growing up feeling like there was something wrong with her because her mom was sick all the time and all her friends' moms seemed happy and healthy and were available to their kids. She yearned for that kind of close relationship with her mom. In our phone coaching session, Melinda connected with that little girl and began to develop a relationship with her. She spoke to her and communicated with compassion, "I understand that you missed out on having a healthy mother and I know how hard that was for you." "I know how you dreamed of her sitting in the stands watching you play softball and that you avoided looking out there because you knew she wasn't there." And "I am here to take care of you now and give you whatever you need to feel safe, comforted and loved."

Melinda's assignment was to connect with this little girl every-day for thirty days and to ask her what she needed that day to feel safe, comforted and loved. After just one week of doing this "Inner Child Connection" process, Melinda was feeling much lighter and happier. Although she couldn't change that she had longed for her mom to be more of a participant in her life, she could take care of herself now and give this little girl what she needed.

As a result of working together, Melinda was finally able after all these years, to forgive her. Her mom passed away fifteen years prior and she often felt guilty that she didn't think loving thoughts when she thought about her mother. Because she had processed the unre-solved emotions, she was able to forgive her and let go of holding onto the anger and resentment she had felt.

Six months after her weekly phone sessions, she called one day to let me know she had "fallen in love" with a warm, caring, and com-passionate man and knew that it was because she had finally forgiven her mother and was able to trust someone to be there for her and love her in the way she always desired.

Insight About Melinda

This is the power of allowing ourselves to identify and feel what we have unconsciously suppressed, often for many years. It is import-ant to realize how much weight these negative emotions have in our psyche and how they literally weigh us down. It is understandable why Melinda would bury her feelings of grief and anger like she did, as she was so young when her mother's illness began. In addition, she didn't have anyone there to help her process her emotions and to help her understand that how she was feeling was normal. As she began to have compassion for herself, as the little girl whose mom was sick and couldn't be there for her, she began to reclaim her power.

She did this by acknowledging the full range of emotions she was experiencing, instead of always defaulting to the feeling of sadness.

Learning that sadness was her default emotion helped her to under-stand herself and what she was experiencing at a deeper level. It taught her to bring consciousness to the emotion of sadness and iden-tify what "avoidance emotions" were present beneath the sadness. Those emotions would then signal what she needed to truly feel in order to heal. And, in addition, what actions she needed to take in order to move past that experience and create something different.

Choosing to Listen

MY SPOTLIGHT

Guilt Taught Me an Invaluable Lesson

My friend Rebecca loves to use guilt to get me to do things. And although I love her dearly, one day it occurred to me that I needed to start looking at why I allowed her to guilt me into attending events I didn't want to attend or doing things I didn't really want to do. As I began exploring my reason for allowing guilt to "work" on me, I dis-covered that my default emotion, guilt, was at play.

As I tried to think about why I was feeling guilty and taking more responsibility for things than I needed to, I saw a new level of my own healing that I needed to address. When I was younger, I was the kid who was always loud, the one who was trying to get attention. And I often received negative attention for it. I was frequently told to be quiet and stop making so much noise. Although that may have been an appropriate response to my loud behavior in the moment, I inter-preted that in a way that made me feel bad about myself. I learned that I had the power to easily upset someone, and that when I did that, I would receive their disapproval. As a result, I always wound up feeling guilty or overly responsible for others' unhappiness.

So now fast-forward thirty years later. My friend who loves to guilt people into doing things and I, who can so easily "feel guilty," go hand in hand, like two peas in a pod. But here is the good news. Once we become aware of our emotions and past history, we can own what is going on. I didn't have to make her "wrong" for trying to make me feel guilty, even though she wasn't doing it consciously. Nor did I have to make myself "wrong" for feeling guilty. I used the experience of "feeling guilty," and the truth that it had begun to feel disingenuous, to uncover an opportunity to heal. And then, of course, that's exactly what I did. I used the experience to heal and to grow.

I connected deeply with this guilt, by using the exercise at the end of this chapter. And I uncovered the deeper emotion underneath the guilt, which was fear. Fear was my avoidance emotion. What I most feared was that I wouldn't be liked and accepted by my friend if I said "no" to her. The little girl within me needed to be accepted and loved and to feel okay with who she was.

As I connected with the little girl, I shared with her that we are okay and I will take care of her no matter what. She doesn't need to please other people to feel at peace with who she is. Communicating and connecting with the little child within us deepens our relationship to ourselves and gives that little child what she needs to feel safe, okay, protected, or whatever it is she may need. Instead of creating conflict with my friend or pointing the finger at her for trying to guilt me into things, I looked inside. This situation, which could have otherwise become a negative experience, gave me the opportunity to embrace another level of my own healing, deepen my relationship with myself, and feel more at peace.

Your default emotion is overbearing and all encompassing. It makes you think it is the real issue. But it is really just masking what needs to be addressed. And when the mask is ripped off, we finally see what is lurking underneath. We see the emotion or emotions that we have been avoiding. And that is where true growth can occur.

Eliza—Successful, Yet Ashamed

Eliza was married, had a great career as the manager of a media advertising sales team and lived in a beautiful home and community. So how could this seemingly put together businesswoman, who looks successful and on top of the world, lose control of herself and her life on a daily basis? Easily. A default emotion was in place and was running the show.

Eliza communicated with me at the beginning of our coaching process that she was ready to get down to the root of something she was extremely ashamed of—her road rage. She was tired of having "incidents" with people in cars on a daily basis and knew that there was something going on within her that was causing these daily outbursts. Transference was definitely taking place, so I began to ask Eliza questions about her past to determine what beliefs or unresolved emotions she was transferring into her current circumstances.

I first asked Eliza to share what she remembered about her childhood. She shared that her mom left when she was a little girl and she was solely raised by her grandparents. As we explored the impact this life-changing event had on her, I asked her to connect with that little girl through the "Inner Child Connection" Process.

"Take a deep breath and allow yourself to see this little girl sitting in front of you," I said.

I had her deeply connect with what this little girl felt when she realized her mom was gone. As difficult as it was, it was important for her to reconnect to herself and how she felt.

I had her ask the little girl this question: "What did it feel like to you when you realized your mom was gone?"

I continued, "Take a deep breath and allow yourself to connect with that feeling."

"Scared," she said, "I felt scared."

I asked her to tell me more and she continued on. "Lost, insecure, like I had no one and nothing to hold onto . . . I think I felt that when she left, she took my safety, security, and comfort with her."

As Eliza continued to describe the effect her mother leaving had on her as a little girl, she shared that she had been waiting most of her life for the other shoe to drop, always feeling like something bad was about to happen. As Eliza connected with the little girl within her that felt insecure and out of control, she could see and understand why she had this pervasive need to be in control of everything in her life and why when she wasn't in control, she felt insecure. But instead of allowing herself to feel insecure at times, which was the emotion she most needed to feel and the one she was most avoiding, she unconsciously chose to cover up the insecurity and out of control feelings with anger. Anger channeled into road rage covered up the feelings of insecurity this little girl didn't want to experience again.

As she continued to share that these feelings of "not being in control" were surfacing a lot at work lately, with her boss's condescending manner and unrealistic demands of her, she started to see exactly why the road rage was taking place. He used sarcasm to deal with the pressure he felt and often called her into his office with a stern demeaning voice. She hated the way he said her name and she felt insignificant when he spoke to her. The more she covered up how she truly felt about the way her boss was treating her, the more she unconsciously needed to find a place for her true feelings to unleash themselves. She felt rage, anger, and injustice at how she was being treated and she longed to feel power and control in her life. She transferred her need for power and control to her drive time.

In a 3,000-pound car, she felt powerful and had perceived control of the situation, even though she was putting herself and others at risk or in harm's way. The reality of the situation didn't matter, because in that moment she was allowing the rage she felt inside, both from the current experiences in her life and all that it was bringing up from her past, to be released.

Like a volcano stirring within, our unexpressed and suppressed emotions will eventually explode. If we aren't conscious of these emotions or don't know how to express them in a healthy way, they will erupt at inappropriate times in places where they don't belong, causing us to potentially hurt ourselves and others.

Eliza's work for the week after our session was to deeply connect with the little girl who felt out of control and comfort her by letting her know that the adult Eliza was going to take care of things now. And before she got into her car, she would communicate to the little girl that the adult Eliza was going to handle the drive in a calm and peaceful way. Eliza's work for the next few months between our weekly sessions was to develop a deeper relationship with this little girl by communicating with her daily and asking her how she was feeling and what she needed to feel safe, secure and in control. All her life, Eliza had felt like she was insignificant. She didn't feel like she was able to speak her truth and didn't feel like she had the control to truly change her life.

Insight About Eliza

By reconnecting with this little girl and listening to her needs as well as comforting her insecurity, Eliza felt more at peace and was able to control her urge to transfer her feelings of rage and anger to others on the road. One of the unexpected events that occurred after working together, was Eliza was offered a new job at a prominent radio station in town. It was no longer aligned with who she was to remain in a position where her boss treated her with disrespect day after day. She accepted the position and was thrilled to have a new boss that was kind, supportive and encouraging instead of demeaning and sarcastic. This new position was possible because Eliza had made peace with the past events that were causing her to attract her previous boss's type of personality into her life.

Counteracting Your Default Emotion

Exploring and understanding your default emotion is an essential component to being able to both make changes in your life and be at peace with how you are feeling. So what can you do when you realize your default emotion is taking over? How do you counteract your default emotion in the moment you discover it's not appropriate for the situation you are in?

You will, of course, want to explore it deeper and do inner work with it at a later time by using the exercise at the end of this step. However, outside of engaging in the inner exploration, here is a simple technique to use to bring more balance and clarity to the situation right away. In the moment you realize that your default emotion is arising, you simply want to connect with the opposite emotion. For example, when something happens that doesn't feel good to you or you hit an obstacle or challenge, your default emotion may be to feel powerlessness like Amanda did. So powerlessness would be your default emotion. Your work then is to practice connecting with the part of you that does feel powerful, and knows that you do have control over some things in your life, and then take action on one thing that is in your control. In other words, allow yourself to see what you do have control over or where you can feel authentically powerful and take action. By doing this, you are connecting with your power and not allowing your powerless feelings to run the show.

Or maybe you have discovered that negativity is your default emotion. You easily become negative when things don't turn out exactly the way you want them to. In the moment you realize you are "being negative" again, connect with the opposite emotion or experience. You may want to connect with something positive or a memory that makes you feel happy. Ask yourself, "What can I do in this moment to focus on something that I feel good, positive, or happy about?" And "What is one thing in this seemingly negative situation that is positive?" Connect with these positive emotions and allow yourself to disconnect from the negativity until you have more time to do some inner work with your negative default emotion.

In this step, we have explored in depth how essential identifying, understanding, and embracing your default emotion is. Now, it's your turn to explore more about your default emotion. Begin by writing down the emotion you feel often and then exercise that emotion with the exercise below. It will give you insight into the wisdom these emotions hold for you.

EXERCISE

Your Turn: Exercise Your Default Emotion

Take your "anxiety" or any other emotion on a walk. Yes, literally, a walk. Put your walking shoes on, go outside, and then just listen. As you listen, identify what this emotion is trying to communicate to you by asking yourself the questions below. You may want to take these questions with you and ask all of them or just keep repeating one of the questions that is most pertinent to your situation and listen for the answers. Trust yourself and begin.

1.   What is this emotion trying to express or communicate to me? How is this emotion trying to get my attention?

2.   Where in your body is that anxiety or emotion creating a sensation? Is there tingling or uneasiness in your stomach, tightness in your chest, or does your throat feel constricted? Breathe into those areas and picture the sensation releasing as you listen to the wisdom this emotion holds.

3.   Is this your anxiety or emotion to feel? Identify if this anxiety belongs to you or maybe you are feeling someone else's anxiety. You could have taken on your spouse's or friend's

anxiety about something he or she is dealing with. Or taken on generational "anxiety," more a way of being that you learned or inherited that didn't originate from you or your life experiences.

4. If it's someone else's, make the declaration to yourself that you will set it down and not take it on anymore. Imagine a beautiful stream or a sacred fire and place the anxiety there, to be released from you and your psyche.

As you continue on your walk, ask any other questions you need the answers to and visualize the emotion being released from your body through your fingertips and out the bottom of your feet. Allow yourself to let it go.

MY SPOTLIGHT

Releasing My Anxiety

I did this recently. I took my "anxiety" on a walk and this is what my anxiety shared: "Relax! Let life be as it is. Focus on what's important to you and let everyone else and everything else work itself out. You can't control it anyway. Bring your energy to all things but not your fear, not your anxiety, not your worry. When you focus on fear and anxiety, you guarantee you will get the very result you don't want. The very result you feared. Let go. Relax. Breathe into the simplicity of all things in your life now. Your daughter, the sun, the wind on your cheeks, your health, breathe it in. Enjoy it. Now is the only moment there is. Anxiety and worry and fear live in the future and are based on the past. Live in this moment and all of that will melt away."

Once I became clear about what my anxiety wanted to communicate with me, the other person and situation I was trying to control just disappeared from my mind. I wasn't even thinking about it anymore. It was like magic; the anxiety just disappeared. Because, remember, it was never about that person in the first place. It was my anxiety being transferred into the relationship and situation.

The Bite-Size exercise and Emotional Default Process that complete this step will guide you to further exploration of your default emotion, the true emotion underneath it, and what you need to do to move past these emotions and experience more of what you want.

Bite-Size Exercise

❖ ❖ ❖

Take a moment right now to write down your default emotion on a blank sheet of paper or in the notes on your smart phone. Over the next three days, make a conscious effort to become the observer of your emotions. Each time you feel your default emotion present, go to that note and write down one sentence about how you felt. For example, "I felt frustrated because I didn't finish my work on time." At the end of the three days, notice how many times your default emotion was present and commit to taking one action to move through that emotion over the following seven days. Maybe you will choose to take that frustration on a walk or journal the expression of it.

Want More? Download a Default Emotion worksheet at www.dianeal-tomare.com/DefaultEmotion

The Emotional Default Process

Take a deep breath, close your eyes, and turn your awareness inside.

1. As you take another deep breath, notice a part of your life, situation, or relationship that you don't feel at peace with. Just acknowledge the feelings you have about it and write them down.

2. As you breathe into these feelings, identify the emotion that is familiar to you—the emotion you experience often. In other words, what is your default emotion? What emotion do you find yourself "going to" often in this experience or in your life in general? Maybe it's anger, powerlessness, frustration, rage, fear, loneliness, guilt, worry, sadness, hurt, laziness, or numbness.

3. Then allow yourself to see what areas of your life you often feel that way in. Maybe it's in your relationships, finances, career, business, health, or most areas of your life

4. Take a deep breath and call forth the little child within you who has experienced this feeling or feelings at other times in your life. For example, the little child that knows the anxiety or fear you may be feeling. Just connect with this child and see this child sitting in front of you.

5. Take a deep breath and ask this child what else she is feeling. Ask the little child what emotion or emotions she is feeling in addition to your default emotion. What is the deeper feeling or feelings that are present? Or what emotion are you most avoiding? Is it anger, powerlessness, frustration, rage, fear, loneliness, worry, sadness, guilt, hurt, or another emotion?

6. Ask this child to give this deeper emotion a voice. If this emotion could speak, what would it say to you or want to express to the person involved in this situation? What is this emotion trying to signal to you or alert you about? Trust whatever answers are coming to you and write them down.

7. Now ask this little child what she most fears will happen. What is his/her greatest fear? What is the worst outcome that could happen in this relationship, situation, or experience?

8. Give this little child permission to notice how this specific event, incident, or experience has caused you to feel this deeper emotion. Take a deep breath as you acknowledge that this emotion is coming from what this child most fears or has experienced in the past.

9. Take this little girl in your arms and communicate with her. Ask her what she needs. Does she need love, certainty, reassurance, to feel safe, or to communicate something to someone?

10. Finally, tell this child you are here now. She doesn't have to bear this burden alone anymore. You, the adult, are here to protect her, to take care of her, to keep her safe and to love her. Ask this little child what that would look like this week. What does she need you to know or to do so that she feels protected and safe? Maybe she wants you to visit with her often, listen to her needs or take time to acknowledge her. Maybe this little child needs extra care or compassion this week. Just listen and trust what she is communicating with you.

Take a deep breath and acknowledge yourself and this little child for all the amazing work you just did! Schedule the actions you received from this exercise in your calendar and visit this wisdom often this week.

Listen to the Voice of
Your Emotions

Have you ever been asked how you're feeling and stumbled to find the right words to express what you truly felt? Maybe you blurted out or thought, "Feeling? Um . . . I'm feeling horrible! This feels really bad and I don't know how to explain it other than to say, make it go away."

For many of us, it is difficult to identify how we are honestly feeling, let alone understand how to process our emotions and release them. In this step, I will share a simple and powerful tool to help you move through even the most difficult emotions. You may not know what emotion you are feeling at the time, but you are probably pretty familiar with the phrases that repeatedly echo in your mind. By connecting with these thoughts and beliefs that may sometimes feel like a broken record, you will be able to more easily describe what the voice of your emotions sounds like and how to use this powerful insight to create what you desire.

The following phrases will no longer haunt you:

- *I'm not good enough.*
- *No one will ever love me.*
- *I don't know what to do.*
- *Nothing ever works out for me.*
- *I just can't take it anymore.*

Instead, you will be able to identify the emotions that are trying to express themselves and finally move past them to create more of what you want.

As we have explored in depth, understanding exactly what we are feeling and what our emotions are trying to tell us is crucial to letting go of the past. And on our journey to creating what we most desire, our emotions can guide us to the places where we are off track and to what degree we are off the path we most need to be on. Our emotions may indicate that we aren't okay with something, or they may alert us to switch course and proceed in a different direction.

Consistently ignoring and avoiding our emotions often leads us to take the path of least resistance and not follow the course that would be the most fulfilling. And on top of that, in the management of our feelings, we often find something outside of ourselves to deal with or handle these built up or pent up emotions and experiences. People often cover up their emotions with food, alcohol, shopping, over-compensating in a relationship, or other vices. By identifying the voices of your emotions and using the Emotional Expression Technique that you will learn in this step, you will be able to move through whatever you are experiencing and devote more of your energy towards taking actions that are aligned with what you want to create in your life instead of pushing down the feelings of the past. You will also be able to focus all your attention on your desired result instead of dealing with the roadblocks that your emotions will eventually put in the way of you accomplishing your goals.

The Voice of Our Emotions

Understanding what our emotions are trying to communicate becomes easier if we give them a voice. Let's explore the voices of a few common emotions. As you read through the following list, circle the ones that most resonate with you.

The voice of anger says:

- ◦ Stop it. Don't do that anymore.
- ◦ Don't allow that anymore.
- ◦ I can't take this anymore.
- ◦ I've had it.
- ◦ I'm not being heard.
- ◦ I'm misunderstood.
- ◦ I'm fed up.

The voice of shame says:

- ◦ I feel bad about who I am.
- ◦ I feel bad about what happened.
- ◦ I am ashamed that I was involved in that.
- ◦ I feel bad about the way that made me feel.
- ◦ I am wrong.
- ◦ There is something wrong with me.
- ◦ I am a bad girl/boy/friend/daughter/spouse.

The voice of guilt says:

- ◦ I'm not a good person.
- ◦ That was wrong.
- ◦ I shouldn't have done that.
- ◦ I should've known better.
- ◦ I did know better.
- ◦ I didn't honor myself.
- ◦ I allowed myself to be violated.
- ◦ I violated someone else.
- ◦ I let them down.

The voice of frustration says:

- ° Things aren't going the way I want them to.
- ° I can't figure this out.
- ° This is too difficult.
- ° I can't do this.
- ° I can't have what I want.
- ° I'm not good enough.
- ° It's not working out the way I want it to.
- ° I'll never get what I want.
- ° Forget it; it doesn't matter anyway.

The voice of worry says:

- ° Something bad is going to happen.
- ° I won't be able to handle what happens.
- ° Everything is falling apart.
- ° I can't get what I so desperately need.

The voice of fear says:

- ° I am not safe.
- ° I can't do this.
- ° I don't have what it takes.
- ° People won't like me.
- ° People will leave me or judge me.
- ° Something bad will happen.
- ° I will lose someone I love.
- ° I will fail.
- ° I'm not good enough.

The voice of negativity says:

- ° Nothing ever works out for me.
- ° Life isn't fair.
- ° Everything is going wrong.
- ° Everything *always* goes wrong.

The voice of exhaustion says:

- ° I can't do this anymore.
- ° I don't have what it takes.
- ° I'm not going to make it.
- ° Maybe I should just give up or give in.

The voice of sadness says:

- ° I'm hurt.
- ° I feel alone.
- ° I don't belong.
- ° I don't know where I fit in.

As you explored the voices of your emotions, maybe you noticed a few phrases that are prevalent in your life. Simply picture these unresolved emotions in your body and psyche as if they are roadblocks.

Imagine that when you set out to start something new, the unresolved emotions and experiences surface and stop you from continuing on in your journey. The emotion or undigested experience puts up a roadblock, just like a stop sign, right in front of you. And often when people hit this roadblock and see this stop sign, they completely abandon the project they were working on or give up on the relationship they are in.

Maybe you are now so deeply entrenched in the pain of a past experience that you can see how these unresolved emotions have distracted you and taken you off the path you were on. Or maybe an emotional roadblock appeared and instead of forging ahead, you used it to prove you couldn't achieve something in your life. For example, Genevieve wanted to share a new endeavor she was embarking on with her boyfriend but felt like she couldn't speak up when the time came to share it with him. She was frustrated that every time she had the opportunity to communicate it to him, she would say something else and put off telling him. Growing up, Genevieve had a stern father who never allowed her to speak her mind. She remembered feeling like she could never say what she was thinking or feeling. All these years later, her inability to express herself and communicate what she believed in was still showing up in her life.

Maybe for you, that roadblock surfaces as a voice in your head telling you that you're stupid, not smart enough, not good enough, or unsuccessful like your brother said you were. Often, we mistake these roadblocks as the truth and allow them to stop us from pressing on or staying committed to our goal. We sometimes mistake these roadblocks as a sign from the universe that we shouldn't continue on in the pursuit of what we originally wanted to create.

A 30-Day Challenge: Lean Into Your Emotions

Your challenge for the next thirty days is to try a different approach with your emotions and observe what happens. For the next thirty days, allow yourself to lean into your emotions. Instead of avoiding how you feel or making yourself "wrong" for feeling the way you do, allow yourself to feel your feelings and identify what insight they hold for you. And then, most importantly, take the action you were going to take prior to feeling that emotion. Instead of using your emotions against yourself as a way to hold you back, break you down, or let fear take control, look at what that emotion is trying to tell you and forge on with your plan of action in spite of that temporary emotional experience.

Engaging in this further exploration of your emotions is extremely valuable, so that you can easily recognize the wisdom of your emotions and become so intimately connected with what they feel like and sound like that you will recognize them when they arise again. As you give your emotions a voice and allow them their needed expression, they will give you immense insight into what is truly going on in your life and will guide you towards what's next.

EXERCISE

The Emotional Expression Technique

So how do you move through these emotions that have been getting in the way of your peace, fulfillment, and happiness? You learn to identify their voices by using this exercise whenever you feel overwhelmed, stuck, aren't moving forward towards your goal, or just feel down. It will help you move through whatever is present.

1. **Observe what's happening.** What is the situation that you are experiencing? Write it out like a story.

2. **Notice what feelings are present.** Notice how this experience feels to you.

3. **Give the feelings a "voice."** Use the "Voices of our Emotions" list to identify the voice of your feelings. And acknowledge if this is a feeling you have experienced in the past.

    As you work through this exercise, you may discover that more than one emotion is present. Identify the voices of each of your emotions and work through the rest of the exercise with each emotion separately.

4. **Allow yourself to feel the feeling and observe where you feel this emotion in your body.** Honor these feelings until they "let go" of you or diminish in some way. And, most importantly, express the emotion in some physical way so you can release it from your body. For example, take a walk, journal, or express the emotion in a yoga or kickboxing class. Find a healthy physical outlet for your emotion.

Once you have completed this exercise, take action! Take one action that is aligned with what you want to create in your life.

The Emotional Expression Technique in Action

Let's look at an example of this technique in action and how I used it to release the roadblocks that were present in my own life.

My husband and daughter absolutely love traveling. Over the summer I had a lot of projects, workshops, and speaking engagements, so they took a few trips without me. I can remember one weekend in particular that was extremely difficult, where I couldn't shake this intense dread and fear that something really bad was going to happen to my daughter. Because this was a challenge I had worked through before, I was familiar with this feeling. But here it was again, so I knew there was another layer of healing that needed to be done.

As I became aware of what I was feeling, my first step was to identify whether this was my intuition telling me that something bad was actually going to happen or whether this was simply a fear from my past being transferred to my current experience. As I sat with the feelings and listened to what my instinct was telling me, clarity about the situation began to emerge. I had the feeling that it was just fear from my past. I also knew that the root of this transference stemmed from early experiences in my life where I was deeply attached to someone and then the person I loved left. I had this fear of loving someone so deeply and then having this person leave me.

And so I had unconsciously built within me this belief that if I really love someone, or the more that I loved them, the more likely it was that this person was going to leave. Remember, our beliefs are our beliefs and they aren't always rational. And, of course, the love for my daughter is so amazing and intense that it makes sense that I would have a fear of losing her. Then when you add my belief that "The people I love leave me," you can see how I would have an intensified fear in place.

My husband and daughter had left early on Friday morning and hadn't been gone for too long. It was Friday at about 4:00 p.m. and I just couldn't bear the feeling any longer. I couldn't shake the visuals that were coming into my head and the panic I was feeling in my chest. What I was experiencing was real. So, I decided to go to yoga to move some of the energy and emotion that was within me. The instructor guided us to close our eyes, take a deep breath, and set an intention for our practice. The intention that came to me was remarkably clear and I heard it immediately. The intention was "to honor my fear of losing my daughter." And so I did that throughout the whole hour-long yoga practice. I used my breath to just "be" with and honor that fear. To acknowledge it and allow it to be there.

I don't know at what moment in the yoga class it lifted. But at some point, I had completely let go of that feeling. It was gone. I wasn't in panic mode any longer. I didn't have the visions of something bad happening and I was totally at peace. Over the next few days while she was out of town, I remained in a state of peace, almost to the point of bliss. I was simply experiencing the events I had planned for that weekend and noticing that the fear didn't surface much. It was a fleeting thought once or twice over the next few days, but that was nothing compared to what I was experiencing prior to this yoga class. This is the magic of honoring our feelings and honoring our truth.

As I honored my feelings in the yoga practice, I saw the connection this fear had to my past. It gave me the clarity I needed to understand how the fear of losing someone I loved was being transferred from my past experiences to my present. Knowing this helped me to have compassion for myself and understand why I would have this intense feeling of panic and anxiety about my daughter being away from me for the weekend. In honoring my experience, allowing it to just be as it was, and not judging myself in any way, I allowed the feelings to move through me, let go of me, and I was free.

Reviewing the Emotional Expression Technique

Let's review how I used the Emotional Expression Technique:

1. **Observe what's happening.** What is the situation that you are experiencing? *I was feeling fear that something bad was going to happen to my daughter.*

2. **Notice what feelings are present.** Notice how this experience feels to you. *I felt a sense of panic and dread. I felt out of control.*

3. **Give the feelings a "voice."** Use the "Voices of Our Emotions" list to identify the voice of your feelings. *Something bad will happen and I will lose someone I love.*

4. **Allow yourself to feel the feeling and observe where you feel this emotion in your body.** Honor these feelings until they "let go" of you or diminish in some way. Journal, take the feelings on a walk, to yoga, on a bike ride, to a kickboxing class, or anything else to physically move them. *I honored the feelings of fear and panic in the yoga class and felt them present in my abdomen and in the area of my heart. By doing this, the emotions eventually lifted and the end result was a feeling of peace.*

E X E R C I S E

Your Turn: Release Any Negative Emotion in Minutes

Now it's your turn. Use the Emotional Expression Technique to explore the freedom you can create in your life by honoring and releasing the negative emotions that may be getting in the way of what you most desire. Keep in mind that this technique is meant to be used as often as you need it. If you are experiencing something troubling or are going through a difficult time in your relationship or life, you can use this technique daily. It will support you in connecting with how you are truly feeling and will give you the insight you need to move through your initial reaction or feelings and honor yourself in a deeper way.

Listening to the Voice of Our Relationships

As we explored in Step 4, our relationships can be our greatest teachers, if we use them as a source of growth as well as a way to identify where we need to heal. I shared how my relationship with my daughter gave me the opportunity to heal, grow, and evolve in my work through the Emotional Expression Technique. Looking at our relationships—even the most difficult relationship in our life—as an opportunity to grow is an amazing way to see what life is trying to teach us. This has, hands down, been one of the most amazing ways I have transformed my own life.

Jack—Mr. Flippant In Relationships

Jack, a fifty-two-year-old attorney, had become the guy who was emotionally unavailable in relationships. He shared that he had recently found someone he really liked and could sense that she was getting fed up with his inability to be honest about his feelings and deeply connect with her. So he decided it was time to stop building those emotional walls.

As we began to talk during our phone session about what happened in his past relationships, Jack shared his fear that "it wasn't safe" to care about someone again because he was so devastated after his last relationship broke up after twelve years. He decided he just couldn't handle any more heartbreak, and so he became flippant in relationships. I asked him how he was acting flippant and what "flippant" looked like in his relationships. He shared that he almost always avoided deep conversations, would change the subject if "serious" talk began and often resorted to humor to keep even the most intimate moments "light." He had convinced himself and most of the women he previously dated, that he didn't care much about relationships. That is, until his new girlfriend, Elizabeth, came into his life.

As I guided Jack to connect with this fear, and identify where in his body it was located, he began to feel it high in his chest and described it as a heavy tingling sensation.

"Breathe into the fear and allow it to just be there as it is," I instructed.

As Jack closed his eyes and tried to do this, I suggested he ask his fear a question: "What are you trying to communicate or express to me?" His fear told him that it was here to protect him. It was protecting him from feeling hurt and grief like he experienced in his last relationship.

"Good," I said. "Now ask it, How can you guide me in this *new* relationship?" After a few minutes, Jack said that his fear told him to proceed cautiously and make sure this relationship was worth the potential risk of loss of love.

After this brief exercise, Jack breathed a huge sigh of relief and said, "Aaah! I get it!" He realized he was on the right track. He was *already* being cautious and taking steps to make sure this was the right person to take a chance on. Rather than continuing to ignore his fear and having it rear its head every step of the way, this communication with his fear taught him that he could trust himself and his instincts.

The power of exploring the voice of his fear was groundbreaking for Jack, as he began to see himself trusting his own emotions again. As he became more trusting of how he was truly feeling and began to honor his fear and acknowledge that he was really okay, he allowed himself to communicate his true feelings to his girlfriend so she understood him better. The more he communicated his true feelings, the safer he felt. And the more he opened up to her, the more connected they both began to feel. Being in this relationship in this new way was feeling really good to Jack.

And six months after we worked together, he proposed to Elizabeth. By letting go of how the past was affecting his new relationship, he had become open to creating exactly what he had always desired. Jack was now confident, carefree and felt alive about his new connection and commitment to Elizabeth.

Insight About Jack

Past relationships can easily stop us from being vulnerable or getting close to someone, as in Jack's story. When you begin a new relationship and the relationships of your past still sit in your psyche unresolved, roadblocks will show up in your new relationship.

You may hear people say, "I never got over that breakup," "I could never let it go," "I will never allow someone in again," or "I will never trust someone again." What they are saying is that they didn't allow themselves to see what that relationship was trying to teach them about themselves and their life. They didn't receive the gift of that experience and fully allow themselves to digest the emotions. So it remains in their psyche as an unresolved experience to be dealt with at a later time. Often a new relationship will be the spark you need to heal whatever is unresolved from the past. It is always our choice as to when we want to deal with our past and receive the lessons it offers.

Regardless of when we make the decision to fully learn the lesson that is in front of us, we can't deny the truth that we are here to learn, evolve, and grow. In order to transform into who we are meant to be, we must look at every situation, experience, and relationship as an opportunity to grow. We will then be open to embracing the lesson that life is trying to teach us and will be able to move on and experience something new. Until we are willing to receive that wisdom, we will continue to experience situations or relationships that trigger the same feelings or unresolved emotions that we felt in the past. Until we are willing and able to receive the lesson that life has for us, we will continue to re-create the patterns of the past.

CLIENT SPOTLIGHT

Kathy's Push-Pull Relationship

Kathy, a thirty-year-old event planner, was in a relationship that was extremely painful to her most of the time. She truly loved her boyfriend but was in a constant state of conflict in her relationship. She fluctuated back and forth between wanting to be with him one minute and pushing him away the next. She was either hot or cold. One minute she would feel loving and affectionate towards him and then just as easily, she would be completely annoyed with him and not want him to touch her or be close. She didn't understand why one moment she could completely enjoy their relationship and connection and the next moment she was in the middle of a heated argument with him. The smallest things could set her off. As we explored Kathy's past and specifically her relationship with her father during our phone session, she discovered that she had unresolved experiences with her dad that were being triggered within her current relationship.

One of the most traumatic events she uncovered with her dad was walking in on him when he was with another woman, a woman who wasn't her mom. In that moment, she decided that men weren't to be trusted. She couldn't trust her dad, and she certainly couldn't trust another man to be faithful to her. She had no idea that this event that occurred twenty years ago was still driving her to push away the men in her life. She would only allow herself to get so close to them and then the roadblock of fear would rear its ugly head and say, "Go back, you can't trust him, men aren't to be trusted." In the moment when the roadblock of fear arrived, Kathy would unconsciously look for something her boyfriend wasn't doing right and create a fight. She would unconsciously search for anything that proved that her fear about men was right. In other words, she was transferring the pain she felt from her dad's infidelity to her current relationship with her boyfriend.

Insight About Kathy

As Kathy became conscious of this cycle of transferring this pain onto her current relationship and learned the lesson this experience had to offer, she was able to begin making different choices and consciously heal from the events of her past. Her intense focus on her boyfriend's actions brought her to the painful realization that she always put others before herself. She cared more about what her boyfriend felt about her than honoring who she was and what she needed.

The lesson she learned through this experience was how important her feelings and needs truly were. Kathy worked daily with the Emotional Expression Technique to identify how she was feeling and used it to move through the feelings that were arising. By doing this instead of transferring her negative feelings and past experiences to her relationship, she became stronger and more connected to herself.

She strengthened her faith in herself and began to believe that no matter what happened in her life or relationship, she would be okay. She also became grateful for the pain she had been feeling, as it was this very experience and challenge in her relationship that prompted her to begin looking at how little she was taking care of herself and what to do to begin honoring herself again.

Kathy was, for the first time in her life, beginning to feel some safety in her relationship. Instead of the up and down, push and pull experience, things were actually pretty steady and solid. She and her boyfriend hadn't had a heated argument in two months and she was allowing herself to really "love" him in ways that she couldn't have imagined before. She brought him surprise lunches to his office once in awhile and noticed how affectionate he would become as a result. She was enjoying the feeling of truly "being" loved and adored by a man. Even though, at times, she felt a bit vulnerable, she knew in those moments how to use the techniques she had learned to do more inner reflection instead of taking it out on her boyfriend and creating distance between them. Kathy was, for the first time, feeling good in love.

The Voice of Fear

Fear is a common emotion and one that often holds us back from creating something new. It is an emotion that we all feel at many different times in our lives and can be triggered in various ways. As we explored in the former stories, fear was being triggered from feelings of loss or heartbreak from the past. One of the other significant places that fear originates from is a lack of control. I often see this with my coaching clients who have been raised in families where someone in the family displayed a sense of being "out of control" with their actions or emotions.

Grace—Avoiding Confrontation At All Costs

I recently worked with Grace, a woman in her late thirties. She had a thriving business in fashion that she wanted to take to the next level. As she began to explore some of the limitations she was currently experiencing in her business, she uncovered one of the places where she was extremely blocked. She felt really uncomfortable with people who raised their voices, were direct or confrontational in their communication, or expressed their emotions in an intense way. She managed many people in her business, and so it was extremely important for her to be able to deal with people expressing all types of emotion.

As we began to explore what was triggering her, Grace saw that her dad was often extremely intense in the way he would emotionally react to situations. He was loud and she remembered him yelling a lot when she was growing up. It was so uncomfortable for her as a young child, and she shared how scared she felt much of the time. Not only did Grace decide that she didn't want to be like that as an adult but also she unconsciously became uncomfortable with people who were intense, loud, or extremely emotional in their communication.

Twenty years later, this discomfort she felt about her father's emotional outbursts was limiting Grace in her business because she couldn't deal with people who would intensely express themselves. When they did, she would try to smooth it over in an attempt to make it go away as quickly as possible. Instead of addressing what that person was having an issue with or what he or she truly wanted to communicate underneath that intensity, Grace would do whatever she could to stop the conversation altogether.

As she began to work through this limitation by connecting with and honoring the feelings of the little girl within her, Grace became more conscious of the places where this block in her ability to communicate with others was present. She was also able to begin healing the little girl within her who experienced those outbursts from her dad. Part of her work was allowing that little girl to understand that she was now an adult and could handle when people were intense, loud, or outspoken.

During one of our sessions she closed her eyes and saw this little girl sitting in front of her. Her little girl's face was sullen and she seemed defeated. Grace asked her, "What did it feel like to have a Dad that was always yelling?" The little girl shared, "Scary. Humiliating. I just wanted it to stop. I felt embarrassed that he acted like that." Grace communicated with this little girl to let her know she no longer had to deal with that fear, humiliation, and embarrassment, and that Grace would be okay and could handle whatever reactions people had. It was important for her to consciously acknowledge to this child, that Grace was no longer a little girl and was now able to deal with people from a place of strength, wisdom, and confidence instead of from her wounded child self.

Insight About Grace

If this limitation had continued, Grace would have been cut off from dealing with a whole group of people, because plenty of people are at times emotionally intense, loud, or confrontational. As the owner of a business, she needed to be able to handle many different types of personalities. Her consciousness of how this past fear was still showing up, gave Grace the insight she needed to take back her power and to grow from these experiences and relationships instead of remaining limited by them. Grace felt on top of the world as a result of the work we did in her sessions. She shared how her new confidence was often noticed by her closest friends and family and they kept saying to her, "What have you done? Something is different about you. You are so much more confident now." Grace would just smile and then share how this reconnection to the little girl within her transformed everything in her life.

The Voice of Negativity

Another common emotional state that can seriously limit us is negativity. Negativity is a way of being for some and is extremely detrimental to being able to create an amazing life, because the person who is perpetuating the negativity is consistently looking for what isn't working in their life.

CLIENT SPOTLIGHT

Hanna—A Force of Negativity

Hanna was a forty-two-year-old divorced nurse, who came to our call displaying an intense amount of emotional negativity. She was even negative in how she spoke about herself and her life. She shared how most things in her life simply weren't working, including her career, as she was recently laid off. As she described her life and the way she saw it, nearly everything was a problem. Nothing was working and everything had a negative spin to it.

As she began exploring the negativity in our session and delving deeper into what other emotions were present, Hanna began to feel what existed underneath the negativity. She was covering up feelings of loss and disappointment from her childhood with this overall state of negativity. Hanna shared how she often felt alone as a child. Her father wasn't around much, and when he was, he seemed distant and unavailable to her. He wasn't much of a communicator and spent most of his time watching TV in his office when he was home.

Her mother was physically present but was dealing with her own emotional issues most of the time and was not the supportive mother that Hanna needed. Hanna remembered her mom being in her room by herself a lot of the time and hated when she would walk in there and close the door behind her. Hanna always knew she wouldn't be back out for hours.

When she began to connect with her loneliness as a child and the deeper feelings of disappointment, she was able to honor the little girl within who didn't get what she needed. Hanna could see that it was easy for her to be negative most of the time because by blaming others, she didn't have to deal with herself or her feelings. Her default emotion of negativity and her tendency to blame others for what was wrong in her life, distracted her from having to look at her true feelings and what was truly being transferred from her past into her current circumstances.

Although it was never her fault that she wasn't tended to as a young child, she could no longer ignore that the loss and disappointment she felt as a child was still surfacing. Hanna had to begin to take care of herself in the way she yearned for as a young child and allow the process of healing to take place so she could create something new. Her first step when we started working together, was to use the Emotional Expression Technique every day to reconnect to how she was truly feeling. Negativity was her default emotion and like a blanket was covering up the true emotions underneath.

The results for Hanna were astonishing, as she began to give her feelings a voice. She uncovered that in addition to the loss and disappointment, anger and rage were present as well. Hanna bought a punching bag and gloves and set it up in her garage so she had a special place for the healthy expression of her rage and anger. Whenever she felt fed up by something that was happening, she would go into the garage and take it out on the punching bag. It was liberating and freeing for her to let go of all the energy of these repressed emotions.

And as she began to express these emotions when they arose in this healthy way, she felt lighter and shared, "I actually feel happy and hopeful again." Two months into our work together, Hanna, with her renewed energy and positive outlook, found a new position that she was genuinely excited about. And it turned out to be much more fulfilling to her than the previous doctor's office she worked at. These days, she was truly living on the positive side of life and woke up every morning genuinely excited about going to work.

Insight About Hanna

You may know someone like this. No matter what they do or what happens, they always have a way of bringing negativity to it. So when Hanna, for example, sits down with someone in a conversation, her viewpoint and way of being is expressed through the emotional state of negativity. So even if something positive happened in her day, she will be focused on and share the negative part, because that is the emotional state she's feeling and is most comfortable with. By using the Emotional Expression Technique and identifying the voice of her negativity, Hanna was able to connect with what she was truly feeling and discover the other emotions that were present as well. As she explored each emotion individually, she was able to move through them instead of allowing them to keep her in an overall negative state of being.

Allow yourself to reflect on this for a moment and see if you know someone like that in your life. Maybe you are that person some of the time—the one who always has a negative attitude. Maybe you know someone in your life who is so stuck in a negative way of being, that even when you point out the positive circumstances, the only thing he or she continues to talk about and focus on is the negative. The only thing they will give attention to is what didn't work out or whatever version of negative they are seeing in that moment.

It is critical to identify and acknowledge the emotional state that we lead with in our daily lives and then connect with the voice of those emotions so we can utilize the wisdom in that emotion instead of being stuck in the initial experience of it. Our emotions have a huge impact on what we are able to create as well as what we are holding ourselves back from being able to accomplish. If we are in the emotional state of negativity, for example, we will continue to create more negativity. If instead we choose to look at what is working in our lives and shift to the emotional state of abundance, we will create more abundant experiences.

Our emotions are an essential part of the energy we bring to every situation, relationship, project, or event. As you begin to use the Emotional Expression Technique and the "voice of your emotions" list, you will become more connected to the emotions that consistently show up for you and will be able to quickly identify the emotional state you are in. As you connect with these emotions, you will have deeper insight into how your emotional state is either supporting you in having what you want or blocking you from creating what you desire. Emotions are an important key to unlocking what is happening in your life right now. Use the exercises below to honor your emotions and begin to transform a part of your life that you desire change in.

Bite-Size Exercise

❖ ❖ ❖

Take a moment right now to write down one thing you will do over the next few days to express your emotions in a healthy way. Maybe you will take your anxiety on a walk, go buy a new journal for the expression of your feelings or find a few songs that express how you are feeling. Schedule one thing you are willing to do by writing it in your calendar now.

Want More? Download the Voice of Your Emotions Worksheet at www.dianealtomare.com/VoiceOfYourEmotions

---

The Emotional Freedom Process

1. Identify an area of your life that you don't feel good about. For example, your career, your home life, your relationship, your weight, or your health.

2. Take a deep breath and allow yourself to connect with the feelings that you are feeling about this part of your life or about an event that recently occurred. Just breathe into those feelings. For example, *I feel angry, sad, frustrated, or worried.*

3. Connect with the feelings that you are feeling about this relationship or situation. Notice the feelings that have been triggered in you. Just breathe into those feelings and observe where in your body they live.

4. On your next breath, give this feeling or emotion a voice. What would this emotion sound like or look like. Ask yourself, "What is the voice of this emotion?" "What is this emotion trying to express or communicate to me?" Use the "Voice of Your Emotions" list to help you identify this voice.

5. On your next breath, allow yourself to see the roadblock that this emotion is creating. Is it keeping you from moving forward in your new relationship? Is it stopping you from staying committed to your new business or career? Is it holding you back from beginning at all? How is it stopping you from creating what you want in this part of your life?

6. Allow this emotion to communicate everything you need to know about how this experience is similar to one you've experienced in the past. Take a deep breath and listen to the voice of this emotion. Is this a familiar feeling? Did you feel

this as a child or at an earlier time in your life? Notice where you felt this feeling before in the past and write it down.

7. Now, on your next breath, see what you would need to do to honor this emotion this week and acknowledge what it's communicating with you. Do you need to journal when this emotion arises? Do you need to express it in some way? For example, go kickboxing and allow your anger to be released. Or turn up some loud angry music and express your anger in that way. How does this emotion need to be expressed in a healthy way this week?

8. On your next breath, affirm for yourself that this emotion needs expression. Make a commitment to yourself that you will take care of yourself in this way this week. Take a deep breath and ask yourself, "How can I honor my emotions and still move forward on my desires?" "What is an action I can take to move forward on what I want to create in this part of my life?"

9. Trust whatever answer you hear. Just breathe into whatever this new consciousness and connection to your emotion is creating within you. Maybe you feel more at peace, more connected, or more loving. Breathe into this and jot down some notes.

Remember to schedule the action steps that arose from this process in your calendar.

Forgive the Pain of the Past

Julie, a forty-three-year-old financial planner, came to our session angry, upset, and fed up with feeling so much negativity in her life. She was unable to get out of the funk she had been feeling for years. She had tried positive thinking, self-help books, and spiritual strategies—she even got a new boyfriend in the hopes that he would make her feel better—but nothing was working.

As I listened to her talk, I noticed a pattern: Julie spent most of her time blaming everyone in her life for how she was feeling and what was happening. I knew forgiveness was what Julie needed to rise beyond the negativity she was feeling.

The moment I said the word "forgiveness," Julie resisted the thought of forgiving the people in her life she was still upset with. She just couldn't see how she could forgive her parents and ex-husband. She didn't feel they deserved it.

This is a huge misconception about forgiveness. Before you skip this and move on to the next chapter, not wanting to even think about completing this step, let me share an important truth with you: Forgiveness doesn't absolve the other person for what they may have done to you.

This is so important that I will say it again. *Forgiveness doesn't absolve the other person for what they may have done to you.*

It does, however, allow you to release the connection of resentment or judgment towards this person and, most importantly, frees you from that negative energy. Forgiveness doesn't nullify what happened to you but it says you don't want to hold onto that negative energy in your body, mind, or heart anymore.

While forgiveness to some people is "The F Word," and is something to be avoided at all costs, it is essential for us to forgive in order to truly let go of the past and create what we want both in the present and the future.

Remember that large, extremely worn, and outdated sack from the coffee shop story in Step 2? If you are still carrying that around, forgiveness is the key to letting go of the rest of that baggage. Even if we aren't acknowledging the resentments or pain of the past, we are still carrying the huge weight and burden of them with us day after day and year after year.

So how do you finally drop that bag and allow the memories, pain, fears, and limitations to be released? You learn how to truly forgive. Forgiveness is not a thought accepted by your mind but a release you feel in your heart. And in this step, you will learn how to give yourself this gift and finally let go of whatever from the past you are either consciously or unconsciously holding onto.

Holding Onto Anger and Resentment

I wasn't surprised that Julie was resistant to the concept of forgiveness. But I knew once she faced her unresolved emotions surrounding both her parents and her ex, forgiveness would begin to feel like a possibility. We can't even *imagine* forgiveness if we haven't first processed and *released* the emotion associated with it. Because Julie hadn't yet worked through her anger and resentment towards these important people in her life, she couldn't see how forgiveness was possible.

We started with her childhood. As she opened up about her past, Julie explained how her entire life she felt a lot of resentment towards her parents for not being there for her. She felt like they focused more on their lives, their new marriages, and what they needed. Regardless of whether she was at her mom or dad's house, she was often left home with the nanny while her parents and their new spouses were out enjoying boating trips, movies, or dinners. She was an only child and the bottom line was that Julie felt abandoned by them as a child. She also shared the anger she felt towards her ex-husband for his infidelity and his continual need while they were getting divorced to be almost boastful about his current relationship and how excited he was about this new woman in his life. He would tell Julie how happy he was and, further, that she should take his advice and find a new man that would make her happy, as happy as his new girlfriend made him feel.

Both of these situations held a lot of pain for Julie. Feeling left behind by her parents created deep hurt in her heart, hurt she had carried for more than thirty years. And when her husband moved on while he was still in his marriage with Julie, it was the ultimate betrayal. But regardless of how painful her experiences had been, the grudges she was holding onto were definitely holding her back, dragging her down, and keeping her stuck in negativity and misery. These relationships, both past and present, were bringing up her wounds and causing her to re-experience the trauma and unresolved emotions.

Instead of taking a hard look at how those experiences could teach her something about herself, she remained focused on what the other people did or didn't do and how damaged she had become as a result. She literally got stuck in the energy of blaming them for who they were and what they did to her.

When we are in the energy of blaming other people, we aren't able to see the lesson of that experience or how that experience might have been a blessing in some way. Once we can see what the experience was here to teach us and accept that lesson, we can move to the place where forgiveness is possible.

As I guided Julie to connect with her anger, she began to see it as a familiar feeling. She noticed how powerful her anger had been throughout her life and how it had always guided her to strive for more, not accept less, and never quit. In fact, one of the things she loved about herself was that she was relentless. She began to revere her anger for how beneficial of an emotion it had been and realized she was deeply in touch with her anger because of how she felt about the injustices in her life and her childhood. As Julie began to be more at peace with being angry, see the benefit of her anger, and allow it the space it needed to be processed, she became less defensive and less in attack mode. From this place, the process of forgiveness was now possible.

By embracing how much these experiences had taught her about herself, Julie was now able to let go of carrying around these resentments. From this space, she was able to do the forgiveness process, which you will have the opportunity to complete at the end of this step. Through this forgiveness process, she released these negative emotions and experiences from her psyche. Instead of focusing so much energy on blaming her parents and ex-husband, she could now use that energy to create the life she truly wanted.

Months later after releasing this inner baggage, Julie began to think about dating again. She had been interested in this really nice man she saw daily at the coffee shop they had both frequented and he often went out of his way to talk to her. Julie made a promise to herself to act more engaged with him the next time he struck up a conversation.

A few days later, they were in the coffee shop in a full blown conversation and out of the blue, he asked her to go out sometime. Julie couldn't believe she actually had a date with a man that she was genuinely interested in. Regardless of how this potential romance would end up, all she knew was that it felt so much better than holding onto the past and living in anger and resentment. Julie went shopping the next day to pick out a new outfit to wear on her date the following weekend. She was beyond excited. A year later, Julie called me and shared that they were still dating and thoroughly enjoying each other's company.

Visualizing Our Resentments

So how destructive are these tiny little grudges and resentments to our relationship? Here is a visual that will help you see this more clearly. Think about someone you are having a hard time forgiving, and as you close your eyes, imagine standing in front of them. You are close to each other with just a small space separating you. Now, imagine taking a piece of chalk and drawing a small circle on the ground between the two of you. Imagine that every time you have a negative judgment about this person, every time you hold onto a resentment about this person, every time you say something negative or judgmental about them or directly to them, every time you choose to not forgive them for what they did or said, negative energy enters the circle of space and the space becomes wider and deeper.

This small circle eventually grows bigger and bigger and creates a larger separation between the two of you, pushing you farther apart. And the father apart you become, the more disconnected you feel. This is exactly what happens, for example, in relationships or marriages after years and years of anger, resentment, and judgments that haven't been resolved. There is an ocean of negative space in between both people in the relationship. Often, because the space is so massive and contains so many unresolved hurts from the past, the couple can't find their way back to each other. One moment and one event at a time, the continual string of resentments and negative energy breaks the bond they once had.

Forgiveness is an essential part of every relationship. It is important to not allow the anger or resentments we feel to become an ocean in which we can't navigate our way back to each other. Forgiveness is a powerful practice that we can utilize in our lives to continually let go of the past and live authentically from the inside out.

A New Definition of Forgiveness

For some of us, forgiveness may feel extremely difficult to attain; however, it is simply a choice to let go and no longer hold onto something that caused us pain or upset. Forgiveness can simply be viewed as "the choice to let go of past hurts." It may be hard for us to let go of those hurts and forgive someone when we feel he or she has wronged us in some way. However, we must remind ourselves that forgiveness is not the act of condoning someone's behavior or letting that person off the hook; it is a choice to not carry that pain around any longer.

Thich Nhat Hanh has often been quoted as saying, "When another person makes you suffer, it is because he suffers deeply within himself, and his suffering is spilling over. He does not need punishment; he needs help." One of the most powerful tools for getting to a place where forgiveness is possible is by choosing to look through the eyes of compassion. Forgiveness becomes easier when we can find compassion for why that person treated us the way they did. By understanding that this person is suffering from something painful that has happened in their life and that this very pain is the source from which they have mistreated you, it will help you to more easily embrace the possibility of forgiveness. By opening up to this possibility and having compassion for their suffering, you make a choice to free yourself from being connected to them and can let go of carrying the resentment around with you.

Remember, the only reason that someone is hurting you is because he or she was hurt. Someone who truly loves himself or herself and feels good about who they are, does not have the need to intentionally hurt you. And it is important to remember that when *we* hurt someone, it is always coming from *our* wounded self. By holding onto the resentment and grudge, we allow someone else's wounds to determine our destiny and we don't allow ourselves to move beyond the hurt and heal. And worse, we choose to remain attached to the painful experience as well as attached to the very person who caused us this pain.

Let's flip our conversation on forgiveness over on its side for a moment and view it through your life and your perspective. Think back to a time in your life when you did something wrong and felt bad about it. Or maybe you remember a time when you wronged someone else in some way. Maybe you did it intentionally because you were hurting and wanted to retaliate, or maybe you found out later that you hurt someone's feelings even though you had no intention of doing so.

Imagine how it would feel if that person held onto a resentment towards you and chose not to forgive you. Imagine if that person, still to this day, when they saw you, thought back to that moment and held a grudge against you, talked negatively about you, or cast negative energy your way. We have all hurt someone at some point in our life. Whether it is intentional or not, we as human beings hurt people just as they hurt us. It is a part of our journey of growth and learning. And the only way to move through these growing pains is through forgiveness. When we give another the grace of forgiveness, we are affirming our desire to feel peace in our life instead of carrying around bitterness or disdain.

When we choose to forgive others or ask for forgiveness for ourselves, we are a part of the healing instead of the hatred. Neither side of this equation is more important than the other. They are both equally essential. When we can let go of holding onto the upsets of the past or holding onto the feelings of being angry or resentful towards someone else, we can experience freedom in our mind, body, and in our heart. We forgive others to let go of re-creating the past. Continuing on with the feelings of hatred or blame keeps us separate and continues the experience of war-like behavior in our relationship with another person. If you truly don't want to stay connected to this person in any way, forgive them and let go of the connection between the two of you. It is the most peaceful way to release your attachment to this negative energy in your life.

Debra—Dependent On Approval

Debra, the owner of a floral shop, was in her fifties and at the end of her rope. She was in a marriage that was verbally and emotionally abusive and was just feeling broken. She repeatedly expressed how unbearable it was and that she "didn't know how this could have happened." She had always been a strong, independent woman in her twenties and thirties and yet, all these years later, she found herself feeling dependent on her husband for approval and love. However, love and approval was far from what she was receiving from him these days. He was often short, dismissive, and condescending and rarely considered her needs in any decision. He treated her more like his servant, than his wife. Sitting in his chair on a Saturday morning, he would yell for coffee and demand that she always cater to his needs. He felt it was her responsibility to take care of him, regardless of the way he treated her. Although he was secretly having a relationship with a younger woman, she just couldn't seem to let him go. She was angrier with herself than she was with him.

I knew that it was time for her to embrace forgiveness, because she was stuck in blaming him for everything he did and, even worse, blaming herself for allowing it. She couldn't seem to "call it quits," as she put it and forsake the thirty years they had spent together.

The most important person for Debra to forgive was herself. Once she could stop beating herself up for "staying too long," she would have more access and connection to her courage and strength and would be able to do the right thing to take care of herself.

Debra shared that she had no idea how she could truly forgive herself for wasting all this precious time with a man who treated her this way and was having an affair with a longtime neighbor friend of theirs. But forgiveness was truly her only ticket to freedom. It was the only way she could release her attachment to what he did or didn't do and start focusing on what she needed to do to heal.

We began the process of forgiveness with an exercise in clarity. I asked Debra to spend the week writing down all the things she was angry at herself for doing, all those things she was still beating herself up for. And next to each one, I asked her to identify the "moment" she remembered feeling that it wasn't okay that she was allowing this or was doing this to herself.

Here is the first item she wrote on her list: "I knew he was having an affair two years ago and I still went to Bermuda with him and acted like everything was okay. I spent a few nights in the bathroom crying into a towel so he wouldn't hear me, and although I felt humiliated, I continued to put on a smile when we were together because I couldn't bear the thought of losing him and the life that we had built together."

I asked Debra to read that out loud. As she started to read, she got choked up and began to cry. Debra was feeling the truth of who she was and what she was reading.

She said, "I know why I've stayed all these years. I just wanted to believe that we could make it through anything and that our love was real. It hurts so bad to know that he's given up and I'm just not there yet; I don't want to give up."

As she began to see the real reason she had stayed, and that it came from a place of love for herself and all she had invested in their life together, she put down the bat and stopped swinging. She began to admire herself for her strength and resilience and for believing that "love conquers all" instead of feeling stupid and calling herself a fool. By doing this exercise and having this realization, she began to have more compassion for herself than hatred. And, most importantly, she began to open up to forgiving herself.

Insight About Debra

As Debra embraced the love she had for herself and worked through the process of forgiveness, she began to feel more able to take action and make the choices in her life she needed to make. She finally accepted that her husband had moved on and was in love with someone else. And she was now able to let him go.

Six months later when I checked in with Debra, she was excited about the possibilities for herself and her new life. For the first time, in longer than she could remember, she was considering herself and her needs first and was feeling exhilarated by her new home, her new freedom and the joy she felt just being her. She loved her morning ritual of getting a cup of coffee for herself and doing a little gardening with music in the background. She was becoming really good at loving herself and tending to her own needs, which was the exact self care she needed.

Checking In

Let's take a moment and step back. You may still be having a really hard time with this. Maybe you were deeply hurt and wounded and your life was forever changed by the violations of someone else. Maybe you're feeling like you can't get to a place where you can connect with the reason that this happened in your life or you can't feel compassion for this person's pain. Every experience of our lives holds the seed of potential for growth. When we are having trouble forgiving someone, we must turn our attention back towards ourselves and connect with what is keeping us from letting go of our connection to that experience, that relationship, and the past. We may find out that there is more wisdom for us to learn as a result of that experience and relationship.

For example, Debra learned so much about herself from her exploration. She learned how resilient she was and how much she believed in love. Until she did this deep exploration, she wasn't able to forgive either her husband or herself. Maybe you are getting to the place where you feel like you are ready to let go, but you simply don't know how to release the hurt you still feel or the anger that still exists.

Most often people have a hard time forgiving someone because they are still holding onto and intently focusing on how much they were hurt or wronged by that person's actions. As true as that may be for you, holding onto your hurts doesn't hurt the other person, it hurts you. Not forgiving them also doesn't hurt the other person, it hurts you.

Emmet Fox states "Resentment, condemnation, anger, and the desire to see someone punished are things that rot your soul, no matter how cleverly you may be disguising them."[5]

Forgiveness doesn't mean someone didn't mistreat you, upset you, or violate you. Forgiveness says you don't want to hold onto that negative energy in your body, mind, or heart anymore. Forgiving others is an act of grace and all it takes to begin is an act of willingness. You may not know how exactly to forgive this person, but just being willing to begin the process of forgiveness is an amazing first step.

Forgiveness Creates a Clear Path to the Future

Let's see what forgiveness looks like in action by using the visual of the open road we explored in Step 6. In a moment, we are going to look at this expansive and open road to the future through the perspective of having forgiven others and ourselves. But first, let's explore what the road looks like when we are holding onto resentments from the past.

Not forgiving ourselves and others creates obstacles on the path ahead. Along the way, these obstacles may show up as rocks, boulders, stoplights, or construction zones. As we have explored, some of these boulders may be from past beliefs that are holding us back or other events that are being transferred from the past. And some of them will be places where we have not forgiven ourselves or others. The inability to forgive or the choice to not forgive places barriers on the road to our future.

So let's say, for example, you have an experience with a co-worker that is not resolved within you, and you are not at peace with this relationship or this person. Let's assume it is someone you see every day. Imagine beginning on your road in the morning with excitement, inspiration, and passion to create something new. As you get to work you see her and feel a twinge of annoyance in your stomach. For some reason, today you keep running into her and thinking about the things you don't like about her and what she said to you. You have lunch with another co-worker and you spend time talking about her and how much you dislike her. With every bit of energy, you focus on the dislike of your co-worker. By doing this, you begin to litter your clear open pathway with pebbles and rocks. The excitement, inspiration, and passion you had at the beginning of the day is now diminishing and turning into frustration and anger. As this dissension with your co-worker increases, the pebbles quickly turn into boulders, creating an obstacle between you and the clear path to your future.

Whether it's in your thoughts or whether it's something that happens to you physically when you see her, you are allowing these obstacles to continue to pop up within you. Sometimes this obstacle will be a negative emotion you feel, or it may be the negativity within you that causes you to not feel good about yourself. Regardless of the form it takes, it will stop you from being in the flow of focusing on what you want to create. It will prevent you from giving all your attention and energy to the project that you are involved in.

If we are unwilling or unable to forgive, we create these pebbles, rocks, boulders, stop signs, or stoplights to stumble over and deal with every step of the way. Take a moment to imagine how quickly this could slow you down on the path to creating what you desire. Think about how quickly it will slow down the momentum you may be creating in your business or the progress you've been making on a project you're working on.

Let's now look at how forgiveness can help you to clear this cluttered road that is filled with anger and resentment toward your co-worker. If you are willing to forgive her and forgive yourself, you will be able to begin to remove those pebbles, rocks, and roadblocks that are on your path. In addition, you won't continue to place new ones on the road to your future. When you look at forgiveness in this way, you can see how essential it is to forgive yourself and forgive others. Not because what they did or said was okay and you condone that behavior, but because you don't want those blocks in your body or psyche. You don't want these current issues becoming obstacles on the road to your future.

Clearing the Road Ahead

So how do we know when it's time to forgive? Anytime we are stuck pointing our finger towards someone and blaming them for how we feel, what is happening to us, or why we can't move forward, we want to look at how *we* are holding onto our attachment to what they did and open up to the possibility of forgiveness.

It is important to remember that forgiveness is not the end result of allowing someone to be right about something. Forgiveness is simply allowing yourself to release the connection of resentment towards that person and allowing yourself and the other person to have a new relationship. Sometimes that may mean that the relationship gets a second chance. Other times, you may decide not to continue in a relationship with that person. Either way, forgiveness is a natural next step once you have identified and learned the lesson that relationship had in store for you. By learning the lesson that relationship afforded you and forgiving them, you ensure that you won't drag unresolved emotions or experiences from this relationship into the future.

When we hold onto something about someone that we didn't like, or something they did to us, it becomes a part of our future experience with them, until we are willing to forgive and let it go. When we continue to hold onto our resentments, we are guaranteeing that this person will always show up in this way from this point forward. We are guaranteeing that we won't be able to have a different experience in this relationship. In other words, we are choosing to continually repeat the past.

Forgiveness is an essential practice in our daily lives. There will continue to be experiences in our lives where we wanted someone to be or act in a way other than they did. There will be times when we get hurt or take something personally. There will be times when we say or do something that may be hurtful to someone else. Or someone may be offended or have an issue with something we said or did. We are always in relationship with people, are fallible, and can't please everyone. Forgiveness is, therefore, crucial for us to learn and practice often.

When we say we're sorry or accept someone else's apology, we are releasing each other from repeating the past. Letting go of the past and creating an open road to our future is the gift forgiveness gives back to us. And what a beautiful gift it is.

Use the Bite-Size exercise and the Forgiveness Process in this step to create freedom in your heart, mind, and body by letting go of whatever experience you may be holding onto.

A Bite-Size Exercise

❖ ❖ ❖

Write down one person you are ready to forgive. Journal for five minutes about all the benefits of letting go of the resentment you have been holding onto. What will you be able to create in your life by accessing the energy that has been tied up with this resentment?

Want More? Download The Forgiveness Process and use it to improve every relationship in your life at www.dianealtomare.com/Forgiveness-Process

The Forgiveness Process

Take a few deep breaths, close your eyes, and bring to mind someone you have been blaming or holding a resentment towards. Write down the answers you hear to the following questions:

1. Begin by picturing yourself facing the other person. Imagine you are as close as you want to be to him or her. Take a deep breath and notice the size of the circle between you. Is it the size of a pool or the size of the ocean? What hurts are most present in that circle between the two of you? What are you most upset about?

2. Is forgiveness an option in this relationship right now or do you still have things to work through before you are ready to forgive this person or ask for forgiveness? (If forgiveness is not an option yet, honor yourself by going back to the exercise at the end of Step 4 where you will be able to receive more insight about this relationship and experience.)

3. Take a deep breath and allow yourself to see the one thing that you most need to forgive them for.

4. What have you learned about yourself as a result of what happened in this relationship? Can you see how you have grown in any way because of what transpired? Are you stronger, more resilient, or maybe you have more compassion for others?

5. Take a deep breath and acknowledge what you have learned or what you now know as a result of this experience with this person. Maybe you realized you have more strength than you knew you had, maybe you have seen a new part of yourself develop as a result of your relationship, or maybe

you have learned to set boundaries or get clarity about who you want to be in your life.

6. Take another deep breath and allow yourself to see one action you could take this week to make peace with a part of this experience. Maybe it's just something you need to do within yourself to let go of focusing so much energy and attention on this relationship or issue. What's one thing you could do to begin to create more of what you want in your life or in this relationship?

7. On your next breath, notice whatever emotion or emotions are still present within you. Breathe into your heart and see the color of that emotion present in your heart—maybe you see red for anger or blue for sadness or green for embarrassment or shame. Allow yourself to breathe into your heart, and as you open up to release this pain and emotion from your heart, say, *I release you and release our negative connection right now in this moment.* And, *I am freeing myself from being connected to you in this way. I let go of holding onto this upset any longer.* Allow yourself to see the negative feelings you feel toward this person releasing from your heart and picture the color you associated with your feelings being transformed into a beautiful white light that fills your mind, body, and heart.

Take a deep breath, acknowledge yourself for doing this work, and schedule the action that you received from this process in your calendar.

Discard Limiting Beliefs

Today, we, as a society seem obsessed with managing our time. From new technology, to life-hacks, to text messaging instead of e-mailing, we all think managing our time is the key element to creating the life we desire.

I have a secret: Managing our time is not the most crucial element to our success and happiness as individuals.

The most important aspect of your life you can manage is your energy and, more specifically, where you are directing it. Part of what contributes to the amount of energy we have—and either supports our direction or depletes us from moving forward—is our beliefs. Our beliefs either align with what we want to create and support us in doing what we want to do or they keep us from taking the necessary actions to achieve what we desire.

In this step, we will explore the beliefs you currently have in place and, most importantly, whether or not they are aligned with what you want to create. If they aren't aligned, our limiting beliefs can detour us or stop us from creating what we want. We will also spend time identifying what beliefs you need to adopt in order to achieve your goals and where in your life you may already possess those beliefs or have them in place. It is essential to ensure that the beliefs that are driving your actions every day are congruent with what you want to create or you will never start living a life that feels right to you.

All of the work we've accomplished in this book, clearing out past emotions, connecting with our inner child, and forgiving the pain of the past, will be wasted if we don't learn to align our thoughts, beliefs, and actions with the new direction we want to go.

When Our Beliefs Prevent Us From Moving Forward

Our beliefs are the first thing we consider, when we set out to do something new.

Yet, like so much else, our beliefs are a result of our past. Some of the beliefs we may transfer from the past include:

- *I can't do it.*
- *I don't know what to do.*
- *I don't know how.*
- *I need someone to take care of me.*
- *I'm not good enough.*
- *There's something wrong with me.*
- *I don't have enough.*
- *There's never enough.*

These beliefs may stem from a series of "failures" in our life, specific events that took place, or from other people we have emulated along the way, like our parents or siblings. We also pick up our beliefs from our culture, our experiences, our upbringing, our pain, and even our successes.

We are, by nature, judgmental beings. We are always moving through life, sifting through our experiences, and making decisions about what we believe and what we will and will not do in the future. If we want to continually expand our options and become more of who we are meant to be, we must be willing to use our experiences to become more open instead of using them to shrink into some version of ourselves with self-imposed limitations in place.

Our beliefs are the narrative in our head that lead us down some paths and not down others. Beliefs in and of themselves are not bad; they are a part of our makeup. But what if our beliefs are not aligned with what we want to create or where we want to go?

If our beliefs are not serving us, we need to kick them to the curb and start filling our minds with what we truly want. I call this step alignment, and it is an essential step to living your life from the inside out, because beliefs often cause us to predetermine the outcome instead of allowing a new experience to unfold.

CLIENT SPOTLIGHT

Marcy—I'm Not Good Enough

Marcy was a strong woman in her early forties. She had many years of success in her marketing career and was proud of most of her accomplishments. There was, however, one experience that she just couldn't seem to let go of. Marcy had been asked to head up one of the groups at her company that was underperforming. This team had once been thriving; however, there were internal issues that were keeping the members of this team from working together effectively. Marcy was appointed to be in charge of this team and help it grow back into the strong team that it used to be. Unfortunately, throughout the time Marcy was in charge of this group, things became worse instead of better. Because of a few political moves that took place in her company's executive team, she was ultimately fired as a result of her inability to rebuild this team.

Marcy just couldn't seem to look at this and use it as a way to grow and evolve. Instead, she established the new belief "I am a failure." And this very belief was holding her back from moving on. Her inability to make sense of what she deemed a failure was preventing her from taking on a similar position or taking another risk.

When she arrived to our session, I shared with her that she was facing a crucial moment of choice. She could either use this new belief, "I'm a failure," as a way to stay stuck and remain in the past or she could look at how this experience could teach her something immensely beneficial that would ultimately help her to create what she truly wanted. Fortunately, Marcy chose to lean into the experience, explore it, and use it. She began by looking at how this experience made her feel and how there were components of it that were being transferred from her past. I asked her to connect with the feeling that was associated with the "I'm a failure" belief. That one was easy for her to connect to, as she was so familiar with her feelings of frustration. I asked her to identify what age she was when she first remembered feeling this frustration. She immediately recounted how defeated she used to feel as a child trying to please her mother who seemed to expect nothing less than perfection. Her mother's expectations were extremely high and Marcy's response as a little girl was initially extreme frustration followed by throwing her hands up in the air. She usually just gave up because she felt like she didn't have what it took to live up to her mother's constant demands.

In her adult life, Marcy was still being controlled by the bar her mother had set. She remembered one of her mother's famous sayings, "There is only one way to do things Marcy, and that's the right way." She could now see that for as long as she could remember, she always felt that "everything had to be perfect" to please her mother and her mother was the one who determined what exactly comprised this unattainable level of perfection. These feelings and experiences from Marcy's past were still running her life and were what triggered her feelings of inadequacy and drove her to easily take on the "I'm a failure" belief.

Marcy had to make a choice to let go of her mother's expectations of her and start to direct her own life. Instead of saying "I can't do it" and giving up when things got too hard or frustrating for her, she had to face her limitations and learn how to work through them. Through our work together, she learned to honor her frustration and not allow it to direct her actions. She learned to lean into that emotion of frustration and recognize that anytime it was present, she was right on top of a moment of choice to either move through it or allow it to hold her back. And she often used the Emotional Expression Technique from Step 6 to move through her frustration instead of allowing it to paralyze her. By bringing consciousness to what was happening within her, Marcy started to feel freedom instead of restriction. As she understood why she was feeling like a failure and, most importantly, that she could choose a new way of looking at what happened, she began to feel hopeful about finding a new position and creating something new and inspiring in her future. The new energy she was feeling catapulted her to actively pursue an opening she heard about at a marketing company she had always admired and revered as one of the top firms. Within three months of working together, Marcy landed that new position and was thrilled with her new beginning.

Insight About Marcy

Any time we are repeating something debilitating from our past, we aren't open to the possibility of growth but are choosing to stay in the familiarity of what we know. As Marcy used this experience to see what needed to be healed from the past and then used it to grow, she became more empowered and in control of her own life.

This "failure" could've held her back if she wasn't willing to do the work she did and look at her experience through the eyes of what she learned. Because she engaged in this inner exploration and healing, this experience became something that helped her to become more of who she was meant to be instead of a negative bump in the road of her past.

Where We Pick Up Beliefs

As we saw in Marcy's story, she adopted the "I'm a failure" belief from the way she interpreted the negative event of losing her job. Some of our beliefs are developed in this way and some of the beliefs we hold are just picked up along the way. We may have taken on one of our parent's beliefs, hearing it said over and over again and adopting it as one of our own. Did you ever hear, "Stop being selfish" or "It's not all about you"? I certainly did. And I remember how bad I felt about myself when I heard both of those phrases and how limiting those beliefs can be when taken to an extreme. I interpreted the belief "it's not okay to be selfish" in a way that was detrimental to me. I felt that it wasn't okay for me to take care of myself or do things that were really important to me, if someone else needed me to do something else. As I got older, I realized how limiting that interpretation and those beliefs truly were.

For some of us, a belief like this has been in our families for generations and is revered as "just the way it is." Often, if we look at that belief, we can see that who we have become as an adult no longer aligns with that outdated belief. Upon further examination, we may realize that we didn't even really believe this "outdated belief" in the first place. Nonetheless, it is something that may be rolling around unconsciously in our thoughts day after day. Bringing consciousness to the beliefs that we've picked up along the way is an important step in being proactive in clearing out the space to create something new in our lives.

CLIENT SPOTLIGHT

Kera—Nobody Can Be Trusted

Kera was twenty-seven-years-old and an artist in the music industry. She was frustrated with her lack of success and felt she should be further along in her career. As we began to explore what beliefs she held that were in opposition to what she wanted, we uncovered something essential that was keeping her from truly having the success she desired.

She began to tell the story of a few experiences she had in her life, where people were less than up front. In fact, they were completely dishonest and most of them intentionally deceived her. She specifically recounted one event where she allowed someone to talk her into spending fourteen thousand dollars on a recording project that ended up being worthless to her. She had felt like a fool because she trusted this person who wound up lying to her about his abilities and the work ethic of the production company. She remembered that day so vividly, as if it was just yesterday and remembered, promising herself she would never be that stupid again. So as a result of these events, she had a belief in place that "No one is to be trusted." This belief was definitely getting in the way of what she wanted to create in her music career.

As she began a new music project and was looking for a production company to work with, she was limiting her options because of her beliefs and her past. Even if she found a company who people assured her was trustworthy, Kera still had doubts. Because she was allowing these beliefs from her past to be transferred into this situation, it was limiting her possibilities and making her feel hopeless and resigned. Although there were trustworthy production companies, she couldn't see that as a possibility. What she needed to explore was whether or not she was willing to open up to a new possibility and let go of her previous experiences and outdated beliefs.

I asked her, "What belief would you need to affirm in order to easily create what you want?"

She shared, "I need to believe that there are people out there who I can trust."

I asked her to look for the times in her life when people did follow through and were trustworthy. As she began to reflect, she remembered a few times where she counted on someone and they actually exceeded her expectations. In fact, one of the biggest breaks she had in her music career was the result of trusting a dear friend to deliver on a promise to share her music with his well-renowned entertainment attorney connection. Her friend had followed through and that attorney had always been forthright and honest with her in all of their business dealings.

Kera's entire countenance brightened as she recounted these stories of people truly coming alongside her and helping her. This was proof that her belief simply wasn't true. She could see that fear was triggering the belief that people weren't trustworthy, because she cared so much about this project. I asked her what action would help her move past that fear when it reared its head. She decided that she would commit to checking the references of the production company and would also allow herself to trust her gut instinct about them.

Insight About Kera

As Kera began to gain clarity around her limiting belief, she realized that she could trust herself to do the necessary due diligence. This outdated belief that "no one is trustworthy" could have stopped her from finding the right production company and kept her from fulfilling her dream project. However, because she was willing to use this experience to explore her past, identify what needed to be healed, and then do the work necessary, she found the perfect production company to work with and her project was an immense success.

EXERCISE

Release Your Limiting Beliefs

Take a deep breath, close your eyes, and begin to explore the answers to these questions:

1. What is something new that I want to create this year?

2. Is there an outdated belief or a belief in opposition to what I want to create? Here is a list of beliefs to explore (your belief may be similar to one of these or you may discover a completely different belief):

> *I can't trust anyone.*
>
> *Life isn't fair.*
>
> *I can't do it.*
>
> *I don't know what to do.*
>
> *I don't know how to do it.*
>
> *I'm just not good at this.*
>
> *I need someone to take care of me.*
>
> *I'm not good enough.*
>
> *There's something wrong with me.*
>
> *I don't have enough.*
>
> *There's never enough.*
>
> *I'm too old.*
>
> *It's too late.*

Allow yourself to see the outdated belief that's in place and examine it. Do you still believe it or do you have evidence that the opposite is also true? If you no longer want to keep this outdated belief, affirm, "This is no longer my belief. I choose to let this go."

3. Ask yourself, "What belief would I need to affirm in order to more easily create what I want?" Explore the following list:

    I can learn a new way of being.

    I do have what it takes.

    I am good enough.

    I am worthy.

    There are people I can trust.

    I am good at a lot of things.

    I have the support I need.

    Everything works out as it is supposed to.

    Every experience is here to support me in becoming more of who I'm meant to be.

4. As you explore your life, can you see experiences from the past where the belief you need to put in place supported you and was present? Write a few of these experiences down and then affirm to yourself, "I put this new belief in its place and I do have evidence of this new belief in my life."

5. Now ask yourself, "What would I need to let go of or stop focusing on in order to allow this new belief to guide me in this project, situation or relationship?" For example, "I am willing to focus on the new belief I have adopted instead of this negative belief. I am willing to give up substantiating this negative belief with proof."

6. Ask yourself, "What's one thing I could do this week to begin to achieve what I want?" For example, "I am committed to taking one small simple action on the project I have wanted to begin."

Jessie—No Way Out of the Job She Hated

When Jessie, a thirty-two-year-old executive assistant, arrived at our first phone coaching session, she started off sharing how she felt completely paralyzed and unable to take action to obtain a new position. She was in a job where she was miserable, hated her boss, and the office setting was depressing to her. She felt stuck and didn't know what to do. She shared how badly she wanted things to change in her life, but just didn't see that it was possible for her. And she began listing all the reasons why everything she had done in the past hadn't worked.

I knew Jessie was holding herself back from seeing new opportunities and that she must have limiting beliefs about what kind of job was possible for her. Because what I saw before me was a competent, intelligent young woman who could have any job she wanted.

I asked her how she felt about working and what came to mind when she thought about the jobs she'd had. Here's what she shared:

- Having a job meant that she had to work in an office.
- Working in an office was miserable and suffocating.
- Every boss she'd had was demanding and condescending.

Because of her beliefs, she was in a space where she couldn't create what she wanted because she was focusing on "what she didn't want." She was focused on the belief that everything in her future would be the same as her past. Even though she needed a job, she couldn't get one because her beliefs were limiting her possibilities. In addition, her beliefs were immobilizing her and were also draining her energy and keeping her from being able to spend the time needed to find her perfect job.

By bringing consciousness to our beliefs, we can see where we are cutting ourselves off from what we truly want to create. As you can see from Jessie's story, she was completely limiting herself from seeing new opportunities and from finding a job that would inspire her. Because she was focusing on her negative beliefs and what she didn't want, she was also preventing herself from finding the job that would be aligned with what she did want to do.

I gave Jessie an assignment. I asked her to write a list of all the things that she was good at and what the ideal work environment would look like, one that would inspire her and support her in bringing those gifts into the workplace. When Jessie came back, she arrived with a long list of attributes and skills that she possessed. She shared that one of the things that happened as a result of this exercise was that she became more connected to how much she did have to offer and realized that her current boss, job, and work environment just weren't aligned with who she was or what she had to contribute. This was a major turning point for her and gave her the clarity she needed to move forward.

Insight About Jessie

Jessie realized that she didn't have to feel bad any longer or blame her boss and company for how miserable she felt. She could see that it just wasn't a good fit with the attributes she possessed and who she authentically was. This gave Jessie the permission she needed to begin looking for a job that was aligned with who she was and what was important to her. She loved fashion and making people look good. Jessie ultimately found an amazing job at one of the fashion companies she had admired for years and, to her amazement, loved her new boss and the creativity of their working environment.

Our beliefs are often deeply ingrained, however, during our sessions, Jessie began to shift all of her limiting beliefs to ones that supported what she truly wanted to experience in her life and career.

Letting Go of Failure

We gather our beliefs from different places at different times in our life. Our beliefs come from our past, our upbringing, our culture, our pain, and our experiences. They are also derived from the things that have worked in our life and the things that haven't worked. Both of these are a matter of perspective and judgment. We may view something in our life and deem it as a "failure," for example. If we were able to look at the big picture perspective of our life and really knew the purpose of that experience, we may find out that it was actually part of what helped us to be successful. It may have helped us to develop a part of our character or some other facet of ourselves that was necessary for our growth. Ultimately, it was a necessary step in the direction of our success. To call it a "failure" is not acknowledging it for the role it played in our journey. And, of course, we never know at what point in our journey we currently are.

In addition, giving an experience that negative connotation doesn't allow us to resolve it or feel at peace with what we experienced, as difficult as it may have been. It then often becomes one of those moments from the past that has the potential to hold us back. And worse, we may transfer it to a future event because it is unresolved and has now created a fear or roadblock within us.

Here is a powerful belief to embrace and is one that I live my life by: "Every single experience that I have been a part of was a necessary piece of the puzzle of my journey. I honor each experience by identifying the lesson that it taught me." You may want to take a moment to embrace a new belief that is important for you to adopt and live by or use the one I just shared.

As we explored in Marcy's story, her belief that she was a failure could've held her back, if she hadn't done the work to explore it more deeply and actually see how it was here to help her grow.

Now it's your turn. Use the following exercise to take one of the beliefs that is limiting you and identify how it is here to help you grow into who you are meant to be and actually support you in moving forward and taking action.

Bite-Size Exercise

❖ ❖ ❖

Write down one belief that you have identified in this step that isn't aligned with what you want to create. Close your eyes, take a deep breath and affirm to yourself, "I now choose to let this belief go." Imagine setting this belief down on the ground next to you and as you do, notice that there is a new belief that is aligned with what you want to create right there in front of you. Pick up that new belief and write it down. Practice saying it out loud seven times every morning for the next thirty days.

Want More? Listen as I guide you through the following exercise on audio. Find the "Success" audio at www.dianealtomare.com/Success

The Success Process

Take a deep breath, close your eyes, and allow yourself some quiet time to reflect on the answer to these questions:

1. What do I want to create or do differently in the next sixty days? For example, I want to begin my yoga certification.

2. What beliefs do I hold about myself or my life that will get in the way of doing that? For example, I don't follow through on anything I start—it's not worth beginning because I won't complete it.

3. Take a deep breath and allow yourself to identify the answer to this question: "Is this my belief or is it someone else's?" If it's someone else's, affirm for yourself, "I now choose to let go of this belief that is no longer serving me."

4. What belief would I need to have in order to create what I want? Your new belief might be: I do finish projects and follow through with things that are important to me. I have proof that I have finished projects that have been important to me.

5. What is one action I could take this week to develop this belief in myself? For example, I will make a realistic goal for myself and follow through with it. I will do yoga three times this week and prove to myself I can follow through with this commitment. I will then pick one action per month that I will commit to and I will work on following through with it. I will begin to create a new relationship with myself and will trust myself to complete the projects I begin.

   Finally take a deep breath and acknowledge all the work you've done, and schedule your actions in your calendar for this upcoming week.

Win the Battle of Faith vs. Fear

D o you ever feel like regardless of what you want, how excited you are about it, and how much of your heart and soul you devote to it, there is something working against you? And often this something shows up in the most critical moments or right as you approach the last leg of completion? Well, you aren't alone. But regardless of how powerfully this force may be working against you, this step will reveal how you can absolutely still powerfully create your future.

Step 9 is about connecting with the part of you that knows who you are and who you are meant to be, even though there is another part of you that may seem to be in opposition. Think about it as if there are two parts of you that aren't always in agreement: The part that wants to be negative, says "this will never work" and intends on doing things exactly the same, and the part of you that deep down has faith in who you are and knows you can create anything you want.

We will spend time in this step using powerful exercises that will help you deepen your connection with the part of you that believes in you and knows you have the power to create an amazing life. Maybe you've already tapped into this part of you in one area of your life, or maybe you've never tapped into this fountain of possibility. Nevertheless, your ability to rely on this part of you will become stronger as you begin to consciously focus more time and attention on this essential connection.

Don't Allow Busyness to Distract
Your Inner Voice

Alora—Moving Beyond the Daily Busyness

Alora, a stay-at-home mom came to our coaching session extremely frustrated. She didn't understand why she wasn't following through with her desire to bring her new photography business into the world and specifically to begin networking and sharing it with other people.

Rather than continue berating herself, I asked Alora to describe her typical day. She began to relate a schedule that was jam-packed with activities. She was always so "busy." But when we dug deeper, she came to realize that few of the activities she busied herself with were moving her forward in her business.

In order to create something new in the world and take risks, we have to connect with that inner voice of faith that knows we can do it and that we have what it takes to create what we want. But often we get distracted from that voice by creating busyness in our lives. Alora had created so much busyness in her life that she didn't give herself time to "hear" her own desires, let alone express them in the world. She was on three committees at her children's school, always focusing on the next home improvement project and struggling to keep up with all the social activities she was invited to.

In many ways, she realized that it was easier for her to remain disconnected from the part of her that truly believed she could be successful at her new business because she also had a lot of fear about starting this new venture and the possibility of failure. Being busy was the excuse she used for not making time to take the necessary steps to begin marketing herself as a photographer. As we worked together during weekly phone sessions, Alora gained the clarity and confidence she needed to begin taking these steps and felt a sense of relief knowing what had been getting in her way.

Alora first discovered that in order to make the changes she desired, she had to acknowledge that she was the only one who was responsible for creating the unnecessary drama and noise in her life. She had to be honest with herself about how she hadn't *chosen* to make it a priority to carve out time for herself and her business. She needed to make space in her day and life so that she could connect with the part of her that believed in this business and knew she could bring it into the world. She needed time to just stop, get quiet, and listen to what was important for her to focus on and do next. She realized that if she continued to stay busy and remain in the "noise" of her current life, she wouldn't be able to see what changes she needed to make—or have the faith to believe she could actually make them.

During our second session together, Alora made a new commitment to herself by writing down two things she would do every day to move forward in her business. She shared, "Everyday, I will take five minutes to envision how my business will look one year from today." And "I will take one action toward marketing my business." After thirty days of this daily commitment, Alora began to feel like her business was a legitimate entity instead of some tucked away dream. After working together over the phone every week for eight months, Alora's business was thriving. She was beyond excited about her daily life and couldn't wait to jump out of bed every morning and begin shooting photos and meeting new clients.

Insight About Alora

Maybe you too can relate to allowing the busyness of your life to distract you from your deepest desires. It can be a constant struggle in our culture to find the time to stop, get quiet, and listen to what's most important. Perhaps because of the busyness and noise in *your* life, your needs and desires are being drowned out. Before you continue on and read another word, allow yourself some time to complete the exercise below and acknowledge what in your life is creating too much busyness or noise. And what you can do differently to carve out some time for what is important to you.

EXERCISE

Your Turn: Recognize the Noise in Your Life

1. What part of my life takes up a lot of my time and energy? For example, my career, my kids, my extended family drama, or dieting.

2. What about that part of my life depletes my energy, creates negative feelings within me, or feeds the "negative" part of me? For example, I spend a lot of time focusing on what I don't like about my job, what I'm doing that's not working, and the feeling that I'm stuck.

3. What do I need to do to be easier on myself or simplify this issue in some way? For example, I need to stop telling myself that I'm going to have to do this forever and start focusing on what I can do to make it better right now.

4. What is my reward for continuing with the same actions and *not* making any changes? For example, I wouldn't have to look at how or why I'm continuing to focus on the negative, complain, and do things that don't align with what I want to create.

5. How would it keep me stuck to continue with these same actions and not make it a priority to learn a new way? For example, I would continue to feel powerless and helpless.

6. What's one thing I am willing to do differently over the next seven days in this part of my life? For example, I will focus on what I can change, making a conscious effort to pay attention to what I'm doing that's working, and what I do enjoy about my job. I also need to remind myself that I have the power to change my circumstances.

The Freedom to Choose

You have arrived at an exciting place in your journey, as you now have the opportunity to embrace this absolute truth in life: we all have the freedom to choose. You wouldn't be reading these pages if there wasn't a part of you that believed that you hold the power to create something different. There is a part of you that knows without a shadow of a doubt that you no longer have to accept the things in your life that aren't working. You have the choice to acknowledge that there is another way to experience your life and there are more exciting options than the ones you may have been living.

Even though you were born into your family of origin, even though you've had the experiences you've had in your life, even though you've picked up certain beliefs or behaviors or continued patterns that don't serve you anymore, you can now choose a new path. You can now choose whether you will continue doing the same thing over and over again or whether you are ready to embrace a new way of being and begin to do something different in your life.

Remember, there is a part of you that knows you have a choice and wants to grow, evolve, and create more in your life. This is the part of you that believes and resonates strongly with what you have been reading. This part of you is powerful, wise, and knows exactly what you are here to do and express in the world.

However, before you continue on in connection with your powerful and brilliant self, let's give credence to and briefly connect with the part of you that wants to be negative or might want to be the victim. Maybe there is a part of you that still feels like life isn't fair or things just aren't going to work out for you. Maybe this part of you is fearful about stepping out and taking a risk of expressing yourself in a new way. Let's be clear in acknowledging that this part of you is also a valid part of your expression. It's important to acknowledge and accept this "negative" part of you and know that even when you are connecting with the positive and powerful part of you, there will be times that this negative voice pops up and tells you "it's not possible," "you can't make changes," or "you won't follow through anyway."

But regardless of what this negative voice may tell you, it's now time to create a deeper bond with the part of you that knows that you have the desire, the hope, and also the power and tenacity to create something different. This part of you will support you, guide you, and direct you to do what you need to do and to go where you need to go. The exercise below will help you build a deeper connection with this part of you.

EXERCISE

Embrace Your Inner Support

Take a few moments to close your eyes, take a few slow deep breaths, and then answer these questions. Give yourself permission to not "think" about the answers but to trust your gut and just write down the first thing that comes to you.

1. What is most important for me to create right now in my life? For example, to fully commit to building the new business I began.

2. What does the voice of the part of me that doesn't have faith in me, and doesn't believe I can do this, say? For example, "I don't have what it takes," "I'm not good enough,"

"I don't know how to begin," "I'm afraid I'll fail," or "what if it doesn't work out?"

3. Take a deep breath and in this moment acknowledge the part of you that doesn't believe you can do it. Just allow this part of you to be there without judging it or making it wrong. And then take another deep breath and connect with the part of you that knows you can have what you want.

4. Take a deep breath and ask yourself, "What does the voice of the part of me that has faith in me and knows that I can do this say about who I am and what I'm capable of?" Remember, before you diminish or discount this voice, acknowledge that you wouldn't have the desire to make changes if there wasn't a part of you that believed it was possible for you. What does the voice of this part of you say? For example, "I can do this," "I have what it takes," "my passion is strong," "I am learning a new way to create what I desire," or "I believe in you."

5. Take a deep breath and breathe into the wisdom and voice of this part of you—the part of you that believes in you and has faith in you. Spend a few moments right now feeling the truth of that wisdom. Look in the mirror and re-read out loud seven times the affirmations and the voice you heard above from number four.

6. On your next breath, close your eyes and visualize an outfit that would represent this part of you, clothing that would help you embody more of this part of you. What could you wear today or sometime this week that would make you feel more connected to the part of you that can accomplish what you want? Maybe you need to go out and buy an outfit that would most align with this part of you.

7.   Most importantly, before completing this exercise, put the affirmations from number four in your phone reminders, up on your wall, or on a computer screensaver.

A Fork in the Road

You are now at the place where it's time to identify what you are willing to do differently. You are at a fork in the road. It's time to decide whether you will make a daily commitment to pay attention to how you are feeling, to acknowledge those feelings, and to do the work to heal the unresolved experiences that are still being triggered from your past. If you are ready to, declare to yourself that you will make a commitment to change the way you approach your life. This new way of being gives you the opportunity to allow yourself to see every experience and every emotion that comes forth as information and guidance. This very guidance will help you determine which direction to go and what you may need to clear from the past in order to create more of what you want.

Take a deep breath and give yourself a moment to reflect on the answers to these questions. As you make these declarations to yourself, write your answers next to each question:

- Am I ready to choose a new daily experience, be conscious of my daily choices, and learn how to be in alignment with what I want to create?

- Am I ready to set up my life to support me in creating what I want?

- Am I ready to make the changes I need to make in my life?

If you answered yes to all three questions, you are ready to forge ahead full speed. With this new way of being, you will be able to live in a place where you are consciously aware of what you are thinking about, what actions you are taking, and how you need to set up your days and weeks to be successful. You will be able to focus your energy intently on creating the space and the support you need in your life to accomplish your goals.

Choice As Your New Best Friend

As we have explored, our choices are essential in determining what we are able to create. In fact, when you desire change in your life, you want to consistently focus your attention on the choices you are making. We all make choices many times each day. We have a lifetime of decisions and choices to make. Many of them are tiny choices and some are monumental decisions that will affect the rest of our lives. Regardless of the size or scope, all of our choices contribute to who we are and where we are in our lives right now.

The most important decision you must make each day is where you will choose to focus your time and more significantly your energy. This decision will determine what you are able to create in your life. Often times, we don't consciously pay attention to how we are choosing to spend our energy. We unconsciously give it away to situations, experiences, or relationships that aren't aligned with what is important to us and what we truly want in that moment. It is essential that we are consistently aware of what we are focusing our attention and energy on, because only then can we consciously create our lives.

MY SPOTLIGHT

Distractions Threaten My Success

I was often faced with this challenge during the writing of this book. It was an exciting time. I had most of the book complete and was feeling fulfilled and at peace with what I had written, but there was still a small portion to finish before the book could be published, and I had some deadlines to meet. I was sitting down to write on one of my scheduled days, and as I was getting settled, all these things that needed my attention started floating around in my head. Nothing was major or needed immediate focus. However, my mind began focusing on the panic and anxiety of each one and I started to get sidetracked.

One of the most common ways to get off track and easily wither away our energy is to allow our distractions to take us off course. In addition, it's easy to get sidetracked in our busy lives. So as I started to notice the challenge I was having in clearing my mind and getting ready to write, I came to that moment where conscious choice was imperative. I had to choose between clearing my mind and being focused on writing my book or allowing the other ten things that needed my attention at some point in the next few days and weeks to distract me. In that moment, because I had the clarity to know what was going on within me and how I was allowing myself to be distracted, I knew I had to choose whether or not to continue on the path of my distractions or shift my focus to writing my book.

Choice is one of the ways that we can regain control over our lives. Once we have become conscious of how we transfer the past into our current experiences, and we are diligent in working with the different techniques and exercises in this book, we will then have the space and ability to turn our focus towards what choice is most aligned for us in any given moment or situation.

As Debbie Ford shares in her book *The Right Questions,* "No action goes unnoticed. We may fool ourselves into believing that our actions do not matter, particularly if we think no one will know or that no one is watching. But all of our choices impact our future."[6] By choosing to continue writing my book, I was choosing something that was aligned with what I wanted to create. The other items that needed my attention would also be completed, but I didn't allow them to continue to take me off track in that moment on that particular day.

We must be willing to look for, pay attention to, and continually release what's in the way of creating what we want. Even as we begin to connect with and focus on our vision on a daily basis, there will be distractions or experiences from our life that pop up and get in the way. But the good news is that we always have the choice as to whether or not we will allow those distractions our time, energy, and attention or if we will rise beyond them and remain focused on creating what we want.

All You Have Is Your Energy

Because we all have a limited amount of energy, if we want to create something new in our lives or change something that's not working, we need to specifically look at how we are using our energy. We simply can't create something new if we are mis-managing our energy or utilizing it in a way that doesn't serve our highest purpose and goals. We need to make sure we aren't simply "giving it away" to situations or problems that aren't working, aren't changing, or aren't getting resolved. One of the major ways we give away our energy is by allowing unresolved emotions to take us on an emotional roller coaster. Let's explore more specifically how giving away your energy, which is your most precious resource, will take you farther away from the accomplishment of your desired goal. And then what you can do to redirect your energy towards achieving what is most important to you.

So how can we become more conscious of how we are spending our precious energy? Most importantly, we can become aware of how we are managing it on a daily basis. Managing your energy means that when you have an issue—a problem that's not being fixed or a stress that continues over and over again in your life—you take the time needed to immediately resolve what's happening within you so you can move on from a clear space. If it's a relationship that would benefit from forgiveness, you can utilize the "Forgiveness Process" at the end of Step 7.

If you aren't feeling worthy or giving yourself the time and attention you need, you may need to check in with your inner child in Step 3 or if you are feeling emotions that you can't move through, or any other obstacles you are experiencing, you can use the Emotional Expression Technique in Step 6 to clear out anything that may currently be in your way. Even if the issue or problem can't be permanently resolved in the moment, you can use these exercises to be at peace with what's happening temporarily. Then, if needed, it can be addressed again at a later time.

What's Your Bucket Filled With?

It is so important to manage our energy on a daily basis and to clear away any distractions that are in the way of being totally focused on what we are doing. Imagine holding a bucket of water and dropping black rocks into that bucket. With each black rock you can see that the bucket has less and less space and becomes congested. So imagine the issue you had with your spouse this morning, imagine the resentment you have with your boss or mother-in-law, imagine looking into the mirror yesterday and judging yourself in some way. Each of these becomes a rock that muddies up the clear space in your life, creating congestion in your body and psyche. You literally become congested with all these "things" that you are not okay with, not at peace with, or don't feel good about.

So in order to create more success, more peace, more abundance, more love, or whatever you desire more of in your life, you must tend to your energy each day, removing the black rocks in your bucket. You must clean out your internal energy so that it is free of resentments, relationships that you don't feel good about, bad feelings you have about yourself or others or anything else that may be weighing you down.

From this new and clear space of energy within you, you can connect with your vision each day and take the actions necessary to accomplish what you want to create. And even when an obstacle or roadblock appears, you can use the tools we've explored to clear it out of the way. This is the experience of ultimate peace and freedom—the knowing that you have within you the ability to both focus on your desired result and take the daily actions needed to get to your desired destination.

Take a deep breath and acknowledge yourself for all the amazing work you have done so far. You are truly on the road to creating all that you desire in your life.

Use this exercise below any time you feel there is a roadblock or obstacle in your way. You can do this exercise in any part of your life and can use it whenever new things surface on your journey toward creating what you desire.

Bite-Size Exercise

❖ ❖ ❖

Take five minutes every morning to deeply connect with the part of you that has faith in you and believes in you. Close your eyes, and allow yourself to feel the encouragement of this part of you and the reason it's important for you to accomplish what you desire in your life and why it's essential to begin now.

When you begin to feel that negative side of you making an appearance, you don't need to be afraid and back down; instead recognize that it's time to reconnect with yourself, remind yourself of the power you have, and choose to connect with the faith you have in where you want to go and who you want to become.

Want More? Listen as I guide you through the following exercise on audio. Find the "Clarity" audio at www.dianealtomare.com/Clarity

The Clarity Process

Take a deep breath, close your eyes, and allow yourself to see a vision of your life as it is right now.

1. Scan your business or career, your relationships, your finances, and your health and well-being. As you get a picture of each part of your life, look for one area that you don't feel good about or just isn't working in some way. Maybe you are seeing that place in your life where you are allowing "what is" to be okay, even though it's really not working for you or doesn't make you feel good. Remember, all these places that aren't working in our life rob us of our energy and weigh us down day after day. They leave us feeling drained and not feeling good about who we are. Give yourself permission to be honest during this exercise and uncover what is in your way.

2. As you begin to notice what is most present in this part of your life, ask yourself the following questions: What am I not dealing with or addressing? Where am I avoiding working through something that is weighing me down? What is the one thing that is bothering me or upsetting me?

3. On your next breath, allow yourself to see or hear the answer to these questions: What am I holding onto in this part of my life that is distracting me or depleting my energy? Where am I feeling hurt, disappointed, frustrated, or angry? Am I holding onto an old way of being, a fear, or a judgment about myself or someone else that is keeping me stuck?

4. On your next breath, let's identify what fear is in place. Ask yourself, "What fear keeps me stuck or keeps me in a place where I am allowing this situation or relationship to continue as it is?" Maybe you fear you're not good enough or smart enough; maybe you fear you will be ridiculed or humiliated or don't have what it takes to stand up for yourself or make changes. What fear is most keeping you from moving forward?

5. On your next breath, allow yourself to see what part of you, you're not acknowledging or embracing—the part of you that could help you handle this issue in your life. Maybe you need to embrace more of your confidence, power, or courage. Maybe you need to spend more time connecting with the part of you that has faith in you, or maybe you need to focus more on knowing that you always deal with whatever comes forward and that you will be okay no matter what happens.

6. What specific action could you take to make a change in this part of your life? What's one thing you could do that would help you feel a little better about yourself or this part of your life and regain focus on what's most important to you? Maybe you will commit to spending 10 minutes every day connecting with the part of you that has faith in you. Or maybe there's someone you need to communicate with, an apology that needs to be made, a boundary that needs to be set, or something or someone you need to stop saying yes to so you can focus more energy on what is most important to you.

    Finally, take a deep breath and acknowledge all the work you just did and schedule your actions in your calendar for this upcoming week.

Unleash the Power of Your Emotions

So much of the work you've done in this book has been dealing with the uncomfortable stuff within, giving it a voice and allowing it to move through you. But in this final step, you will learn how to utilize all of the energy of your emotions to truly usher you forward into a life that is authentic and fulfilling.

Now that we've tackled the challenge of looking inside, the past isn't in the driver's seat anymore. *You* are. You and the beautiful myriad of emotions inside you that you've learned to listen to and have welcomed as a guide to help you get where you want to go. Doesn't that feel good? Take a deep breath and a moment to fully acknowledge all the work you've done so far.

There's no need to feel stuck any longer. You've learned how to embrace whatever may come forth and do so in the moment, rather than days, weeks, months, or years later. Take a moment to acknowledge this openness within you and how amazingly free it feels.

You are now living from the inside out—being true to yourself, your experiences and your dreams. Instead of hiding from the past, you are now able to use the experiences of your past to create an amazing future. Your past now becomes the catalyst to help you powerfully contribute your unique gift to the world. And you no longer fear your emotions because you recognize them as a gift. This is the beginning of an authentic life.

As you have explored in depth in the past nine steps, transferring events from your past can be limiting; however, in this step, I am going to share with you how the transferring of these very emotions and experiences can also be seen in a different light. I am going to show you how you can use even the most negative emotions to assist you in creating what you want, instead of allowing them to limit you or stop you. Let's look at how this works.

MY SPOTLIGHT

Putting My Anxiety to Work

At the beginning of the year, I was planning to attend a big event. It was a one of a kind experience, but as the event drew closer all I could think about was how anxious I felt, because I didn't know what to expect. I was excited and couldn't wait to attend this event, but was still anxious as it would be a weekend full of the unknown. There would be many new people to meet and many of them were people I deeply admired. Instead of allowing the anxiety I was feeling to hold me captive, I used that energy and funneled it into creating something productive in my business.

I literally put the energy of my anxiety to work. I focused on the details of an upcoming presentation I was giving at a large corporation in two months and set a goal for myself to finish the presentation by the end of the day. And then I funneled all of my energy into that presentation. Any time I began to think of my anxiety about the upcoming event, I refocused my energy toward the next detail that needed my attention. I let myself become immersed in the perfection of it, as I rehearsed it over and over again. I allowed myself to get lost in the details of making it a huge success instead of wasting my energy obsessing about the unknown.

In other words, I used positive transference to find a project to work on that would excite and inspire me—a place where I could funnel all my energy, focus, and attention instead of worrying about and indulging in the anxiety of an event that hadn't yet occurred. I took the intense energy of anxiety and fear and used it to fuel the excitement and passion I had for the project I was working on.

Insight About My Anxiety

We can either use our energy or allow it to use us. Instead of allowing emotions such as anger or frustration to keep us from moving forward in our lives, we can use them as fuel to drive our projects and propel us into action. Take the energy of anger, for example. Isn't there an intense flow of energy within you when you feel angry? The energy can be almost explosive at times. What if you used that energy to do something amazing? What if you utilized that energy to make a huge difference in your life or in the lives of others? What if the next time you got angry about an injustice, you took action and positively affected your life and the lives of others by contributing a solution to the problem?

If you are willing, today can be a day that you draw a demarcation in the sand. A declaration that you will become conscious of your emotions and use the energy of what's within those emotions to drive you to create something new, instead of allowing them to stop you dead in your tracks and paralyze you.

Use Your Fear

I was recently leading a workshop and a woman named Claire raised her hand because she wanted to share something she was struggling with. She had just embarked on an amazing new business venture selling her unique one of a kind art pieces to dealers around the world. Although she knew it was totally aligned with who she was and knew that it would ultimately be successful, she was worried about her financial security in the here and now. She shared how she was experiencing intense fear about her finances at moments and wondered how she could get rid of that fear.

I shared with her that as she had already been experiencing, the fear would continue to come in and out of her consciousness as she traveled on her journey to creating her new business. We then discussed that this was the place where she needed to draw that demarcation in the sand. This was the place where she needed to make a daily or sometimes moment by moment choice. She could consciously choose to powerfully use the energy of that fear instead of allowing it to use her. She could choose to use her fear to alert her when she wasn't in a place of taking action. Then, most importantly, she could choose to transfer the energy of that fear into taking action in her business.

So, during the workshop, she created a phrase that would alert her when her fear was taking over and remind her to take action instead of allowing the fear to control her. Her phrase was, "Fear is present and I choose to step into action." After she said that phrase, she would then go to the list of actions she created at the workshop. This list comprised ten different actions that were aligned with what she wanted to create in her business. She would pick one of those actions and dive into the completion of it. By doing this, every time the fear arose, she was acknowledging both to herself and her fear that ultimately she had the power of choice and was choosing to take action instead of allowing the fear to hold her back.

Think about your fear for a moment. Allow yourself to recall a time when you felt fearful. Fear is a powerful emotion and definitely has physical ways of manifesting itself. Maybe when you feel fear, you have butterflies in your stomach. Or maybe you clench your jaw or your hands sweat. Imagine that you could use that "extra" energy that is showing up in your body and transfer it to something else, something positive, and something to help you get what you want. Allow yourself to see what the fear is trying to tell you. Maybe your fear is alerting you that you are not doing the things that are most important to you. Maybe it is reminding you that you are approaching a deadline and you need to get moving and accomplish something specific. Allow yourself to use the energy of your fear and just like Claire did, create a phrase that will spring you into action and move you toward the accomplishment of your greatest desires instead of letting the fear immobilize you.

Here's a simple example of how to use energy to accomplish what you want. In my household, my husband and I like things clean and organized. And lucky for us, we both have this innate habit of cleaning when we are frustrated, angry, or can't resolve what is going on in the moment. It has become something we just do. When there is a point of contention or argument we can't resolve, we both naturally start to clean. We use the energy of frustration or angst—or whatever emotion is present—to clean the house or take action on a home project that isn't complete. By doing this, we are allowing the energy to move and giving it a place to be released. Most often, at the end of that cleaning session, we are both in a clearer space and in a place where resolution is more possible than it was prior to our cleaning session.

You too can create a practice or a way of allowing the energy of your emotions to move through you. You can create something positive in your life with the energy of your emotions, whether it's simply a clean house or something as complex as starting a business. It has been a great practice to have in our household and has enabled us to move energy instead of allowing it to be bottled up or leaving it to simmer under the surface. There is often a small adjustment we need to make in order to use the energy of our emotions to accomplish what we desire instead of allowing it to hold us back.

Creating Amazing Results

Many people throughout history have persevered and used their struggles to become stronger. There are amazing stories of people who have proved to themselves and showed the world that they could create something extraordinary with their lives despite their circumstances. And don't we all love to hear those stories? Most of us love to hear the details of exactly how they did it and how they were able to rise beyond their difficulties. It gives us inspiration and hope. So how do people create extraordinary opportunities even in the most difficult of circumstances? They do it by transferring the energy of their negative emotions or experiences and using that energy as fuel to drive them to intensely focus on what they truly want. By doing so, they create their own success.

You too can use transference in a positive way and consciously use the energy of your frustration, anger, or other emotions to drive you to do what's necessary to excel and succeed. Think of the times when you've been "knocked down" or "passed over" and allow yourself to feel the physical experience those feelings create in your body. That energy can be used as the fuel you need to drive you to create what you want.

Maybe you've already done this and haven't even noticed. Maybe you've had the experience where you felt "less than" or "not good enough" or "not successful" in an area of your life, and you used that very anger, frustration, or fear as motivation to take action and make a difference. In essence, you are transferring your anger in a positive way into a situation in order to affect change. When we are conscious of our emotions and what they are calling us or driving us to do, we can see these negative experiences in our life in a positive light and use them to ultimately create what we desire. When we don't channel or acknowledge that energy, that's when it drags us down.

MY SPOTLIGHT

Negativity Shaped Me

When I was younger, I had an experience with someone close to me who was extremely negative much of the time. It pained me so greatly to see this person suffer in this way. This wasn't a conscious decision I made at the time, but upon reflection years later, I realized I made a decision at some point about how I was going to react to this constant negativity. I unconsciously chose to always look for ways to find the positive in every situation, regardless of how negative things appeared. I would always negate my relative's negative comment with a, "Yes, but look at the bright side" or "Yes, I can see that, but the good news is . . . " I developed this amazing ability, much like we develop strong muscles, to always see the positive in everyone and in any situation.

To this day, I have transferred this ability to always see the good in almost everything I do and in most of the places in my life. It helps me to see the best in people and to always see a higher place of being for my clients. You can say that I chose at an early age to transfer my frustration and sadness for this constant negativity into proving that there is good in everyone and in every situation.

Karin—Difficulties Drove Her Success

When my client Karin, a thirty-six-year-old business owner, arrived on our first coaching call, I knew there was something quite remarkable about her. She had those qualities that extraordinary people have, people who have transformed even the darkest of situations. She was unstoppable. She was relentless. And she was a survivor. She wouldn't allow anything, anyone, or any obstacle to hold her back. She was motivated and she was driven to succeed, and that was the way it was and would be for her. The most extraordinary thing about her was that this drive and relentless nature came from her pain and her past. It wasn't a quality she learned as a child or something that her parents helped her develop. It was a quality she developed on her own through the hard knocks of her life.

Her parents divorced early in her life and she was often alone as a result. She shared with me how she used food to comfort herself. After school, she was frequently by herself in a quiet, empty kitchen making sandwiches to soothe her broken heart, even though what she desperately needed was love and attention. She told me that she used to jump in terror at every little sound the house would make. As a little girl, Karin was scared and alone.

But instead of accepting mediocrity in her life because of her childhood, Karin used that pain to drive her to help other people succeed. She chose to use that very pain, and her feelings of being "less than," as a motivation to be successful and win. She chose to prove to everyone in her life who told her she couldn't do it that they were wrong. She chose to drive herself to greatness and major accomplishments simply because she wanted to prove to herself that she was good enough.

Insight About Karin

Karin worked hard to embrace the pain of her past and became a powerful motivator to everyone around her. She worked diligently to move from feeling like she was alone and had nothing to creating and leading a powerful team of one hundred people in a company she loved and believed in.

You can do this, too. You have within you the energy you need in order to create what your soul is yearning for you to express in the world. You can absolutely have what you want if you will identify and harness all of your energy into the creation of it.

Use the Place Where You Are Successful

Not only can we transfer the energy of our negative experiences and emotions to drive and fuel our future, but we can also consciously train ourselves to transfer our positive traits and experiences from one part of our life to another. So, for example, if we are extremely successful in business, we can look at what we would need to transfer from that part of our lives into our relationships in order to have more success in our relationships. Most people have an area of their life where they struggle. It is often the area where many of their issues from the past are surfacing. They might lose "who they are" in that area. Or lose confidence in their ability to handle that area. Let's look at how you can take "who you are" in the most successful area of your life and transfer that to the least satisfying part of your life. By doing this, you will feel balanced, fulfilled, and enjoy your life as a whole.

Scott—Finally Tackles Lack of Confidence

Scott's story illustrates how simple this practice can be. Scott was a forty-six-year-old successful businessman and was at the top of his career. He had been rebuilding troubled companies for twenty years. He was the guy that had a knack for seeing clearly what was missing within a broken system and making the necessary changes to make the company thrive. While at work, he felt powerful, confident, and at ease. One of his most difficult challenges was how he felt at home. With his wife and kids, he felt powerless and unable to affect their home life with the same confidence and power he had at work. He shared that he often felt like he was just visiting; like the culture and rhythm of the family was set and he just needed to conform to how things were.

In our phone session, Scott engaged in a simple exercise that opened his eyes to a whole new world of possibilities. During a process, I asked him what he did at work that gave him confidence. He shared that he absolutely knew without a doubt what he was doing and trusted his decisions and his ability in his work. We then used the simple concept of transference to look at what he was doing at work that he wasn't yet doing at home. One of the things he discovered was that at work he was totally involved and engaged in what was going on. At home, he felt like a visitor and was more passive in his home life than he really wanted to be.

I asked him what he would need to do to be more involved at home. He shared that he wanted to have a more active role in his home life by taking the kids and his wife to different events that were important to him. In doing so, he would be able to share more of his interests and bring more of who he was into the family dynamic. His first outing with the family was a Major League Baseball game. Scott loved baseball as a kid and wanted to share that passion with his kids. To Scott's delight, they absolutely loved it and at the game, he felt alive and a part of the family.

Insight About Scott

As Scott began to take these simple actions over the subsequent weeks, he felt more a part of his home life and more confident in his ability to have a positive effect on their daily experience. Making these changes was a lot simpler than Scott originally thought it would be and it made a huge difference in how he felt at home around his family, as well as their connection to him. He was now an active participant in all areas of his life.

EXERCISE

Your Turn: Use Positive Transference

1. Take a moment to identify one area of your life that you feel successful in.

2. Ask yourself what qualities you exhibit in that part of your life that make you feel successful.

3. Next, identify one area of your life where you are struggling.

4. Allow yourself to see one thing or one quality you could transfer from the successful area of your life to the part of your life you are struggling with.

5. What is one thing you could do differently in this part of your life this week?

AJ—Challenged with Discipline

AJ, a forty-three-year-old sales professional, began working with me because of his desire to lose weight. He had a difficult time keeping his weight off and making healthy food choices and nothing he had tried in the past worked. He was very busy with his career and was constantly on the run, often leaving his house at 6 a.m. and not returning until 7 p.m. As we began to explore the area of his life that he was successful in, he noticed that some of the attributes he exhibited at work were not being displayed in the area of his health. He instantly saw how he was disciplined and focused at work and always made sure he was prepared and on top of what his clients needed. He then looked at how that same dedication and focus was lacking in the area of his health. He felt lazy about his workouts and didn't plan or prepare his food ahead of time.

During one of our initial sessions, he made a new commitment to himself and declared that for the next four weeks, he would bring this same discipline to his health goals. He committed to preparing his food daily and setting aside one hour per day, five days a week, for his workouts, even though he had a full schedule.

When he arrived at his session the following week, he shared how much more in control of his life and health he felt. He could see that just by bringing more discipline and focus to the area of his health that he was able to make some significant changes in a short period of time. He started to feel more energy during the day and was sleeping better at night. He also felt more confident about himself in every part of his life.

Although there was still some emotional work to be done in the area of his health, he was off to a great start by taking responsibility for how he could immediately bring more discipline into this part of his life. Now that he had begun to see some progress as a result of bringing more discipline into his health regime, we could begin to focus on the inner limitations that were present.

During one of our sessions, AJ realized that he was an emotional eater. In the moments, when he felt stressed or feared he couldn't live up to someone else's expectations, he would comfort himself with food. His initial reaction to avoid or cover up what he was feeling, was the focus of our work together in our remaining sessions.

Over the next few months, AJ learned how to acknowledge what he was feeling in any moment and embrace and garner the insight his emotion was providing him, through the Emotional Expression Technique. As a result, he began to feel much more connected to himself, how he was doing and what he truly needed.

Insight About AJ

Instead of using food to soothe a difficult experience or feeling, AJ learned how to be okay with each emotion as it was. Throughout the time we worked together, AJ lost forty pounds of weight and as he declared, "I've also lost at least fifty pounds of emotional baggage as well." He was feeling like a new man; he was confident, fit, and as he shared, "at the top of his game in every area of his life." His weight was no longer a part of his life that he felt ashamed about.

> ## Bite-Size Exercise
>
> ❖   ❖   ❖
>
> *Write a list of five actions that are aligned with what you want to create. Directly below that list, create a phrase that will alert you when fear is present and is threatening to take over. For example, "Fear is present; however, I choose to step into action anyway." Whenever you feel fear is getting in the way of taking action, repeat this phrase and go to your list, step into the power of choice and take action anyway.*

Want More? Download The Awakened Process worksheet at www.dianealtomare.com/AwakenedProcess

The Awakened Process

Take a few deep breaths, close your eyes, and allow yourself some quiet time to reflect.

1. Write down the answers to these questions:

    o "What do I want to create in my life?"

    o "What do I want to change in the world?"

    o "What do I see in the world that pains me greatly that I want to change?"

    o "If I could create something that is meaningful to me, what would that be?"

2. Allow yourself to connect with the feelings you would feel if you accomplished this. Just breathe into those feelings.

3. On your next breath, notice the little child within you that wants you to use the pain from your life to create something extraordinary. What could you create in your life or in the world to honor this child within you? For example, I hate to see people suffer and I want to help people heal.

4. Allow this little child to sit in your lap and let him/her communicate all the feelings he/she has about this vision. Take a deep breath and listen from your heart. Listen to all he/she has to say and wants to communicate.

5. Ask this little child what you have learned or who you have become that can help you create this in your life or in the world. Maybe your pain has taught you a level of compassion that is necessary to help others heal.

6. Ask this little child, "What is one small action I can take this week to begin to put my attention and focus on this vision?" Maybe you can re-read your answers to this exercise and feel the inspiration that comes from your vision and what you want to create.

   Remember to put your action step in your calendar so you can complete the action he/she requested of you.

Conclusion

Congratulations on all the work you have just done!

Step by step, week after week and year after year of clearing out negative energy, letting go of the past, and taking actions that are aligned with the new future you want to create, is how you can ultimately create an authentic life where you live your life from the inside out.

Let today be a commitment to a new beginning—the day you transform how you approach the amazing life you live!

Acknowledgments

From the deepest place in my heart, I thank everyone who has supported me and contributed to this book. Words can't express the immense gratitude I feel.

To Arielle Ford and Brian Hilliard, thank you from the bottom of my heart, for your generosity and your huge contribution to bringing this book into the world. I cherish you and your love, support, and divine wisdom more than you can ever know.

To Debbie Ford, this book is here, because of you. I miss you, your unconditional love and the way you always lit the way for me to be more of who I am.

To Susan Harrow, your contribution has been beyond profound. Thank you for helping me be intentional with my communication and message.

To my brilliant editors, Nancy Sugihara, Cynthia DiTiberio, and Lara Asher for your amazing direction and for helping me to dig deep and bring forth the very best I had. Even in the moments I thought I'd given enough, you gently nudged me to garner even more.

To Kenzi Sugihara, Kenichi Sugihara, and the amazing staff at SelectBooks for your talent and immense dedication to this book.

To my agent, Bill Gladstone, for your patience and belief in my work.

To Marci Shimoff for your generosity. Thank you for paving the way and being an inspiration.

To Nancy Levin for your guidance, encouragement, and light.

To Lisa Breckenridge, for your unwavering support and love.

To Stacey Crnich, my photographer, for your dear friendship and for helping me relax in front of a camera. Your spirit is immense.

To every one of my clients . . . you truly made this possible, as you shared your life, your struggles, and your biggest dreams with me over the past 15 years. Thank you for inspiring me to bring this wisdom into the world.

To Jeffrey Malone, Clifford Edwards, Donna Lipman, & Anne Browning for your love, support, and immense contribution to my growth.

To Julie Stroud, Fran Fusco and Kelley Kosow for continuing the work of the Ford Institute of Integrative Coaching and keeping us all connected. I am forever grateful to you.

To Danielle and Michael Guren, my dearest friends and confidants, for all the late night laughs—I cherish every single one of them. You are family to me.

To Mary Lou Yoch, for going above and beyond to support this book in the divine ways that you did.

To Coco Owchar, for your generous spirit and for always being an inspiration.

To my Aunt Margaret, for the way you always made me feel loved, accepted, and at home. I miss you.

To Steve Newman, for saying, "Do what you love . . .nothing else matters." You gave me the most poignant piece of advice I ever received. It truly directed my journey and my life, and led me to find the happiness and fulfillment I was always striving for.

To my family, my Mom, Dad, and Sister, we all weathered this storm together and have remained all these years, still family . . . that alone, says so much. I love you.

To my husband and best friend, Christopher, for your never-ending support and love through the pursuit of my biggest dreams. And to Alexandra—my sweet baby girl, you continually inspire me to grow, expand, and become a better "me." I'm the luckiest girl to be both of yours. You have my heart.

Endnotes

1. Eckhart Tolle, *The Power of Now* (Namaste Publishing, 2004), p. 64.

2. http://www.nydailynews.com/entertainment/gossip/matthew-perry-opens-drug-alcohol-addiction-friends-era-article-1.1388218.

3. http://www.huffingtonpost.com/2014/02/06/celebrities-drug-addiction_n_4740146.html.

4. John Bradshaw, *Healing the Shame That Binds You* (Health Communications, 2005), p. 46.

5. Emmet Fox, *Make Your Life Worthwhile* (Harper Collins, 2010), p. 28.

6. Debbie Ford, *The Right Questions: Ten Essential Questions to Guide You to an Extraordinary Life* (HarperOne, 2004), p. 9.

Recommended Reading List

The Dark Side of the Light Chasers by Debbie Ford

Debbie Ford was an expert in the field of personal transformation, best known for her groundbreaking work on the shadow. She wrote nine powerful books on learning to love, trust, and embrace all of who we are. She also created The Shadow Process Workshop, a three day, heart-opening experience that will teach you how to love yourself unconditionally and will change your life.

www.thefordinstitute.com/shadowprocess

———

Turn Your Mate into Your Soulmate by Arielle Ford

Arielle Ford is a love and relationship expert and has been called "The Cupid of Consciousness" and "The Fairy Godmother of Love." She has written ten remarkable books on love, relationships, and attracting your soulmate.

www.arielleford.com

———

Nature's Diet by Andrew Iverson, ND

Dr. Andrew Iverson is a Naturopathic Doctor, family practitioner and the author of three life-changing books on how to heal your body and stay healthy. His practice is in Tacoma, WA.

www.tacomahealth.net

———

Jump . . . And Your Life Will Appear by Nancy Levin

Nancy Levin is an Integrative Coach and has written two amazing books on how to live in alignment with your own truth and desires.

www.nancylevin.com

———

Happy for No Reason by Marci Shimoff

Marci Shimoff is an expert on happiness, success, and the law of attraction and is the woman's face of the biggest self-help book phenomenon in history, *Chicken Soup for the Soul.*

www.happyfornoreason.com

About the Author

Photo by Stacey Crnich

DIANE ALTOMARE is an Integrative Life Coach and a highly sought after speaker who has spoken at many events around the country. She is often a guest on radio shows, has been featured on iHeartRadio, and is a contributor to FinerMinds. Known as "the coach with the authentic, gentle, and laser-focused approach," she has a gift for nailing the deep truth behind any situation.

Diane has spent fifteen years as a speaker and coach, teaching people how to stop covering up their pain and instead acknowledge it, embrace it, and let it go so they can move beyond a limiting past to an inspiring and fulfilling future.

Diane received her certification and extensive training as a Master Level Certified Coach from the Ford Institute of Integrative Coaching and holds a Bachelor of Arts in Interdisciplinary Studies from the University of South Carolina. She splits her time between sunny Southern California and rainy Seattle, which she describes as the best of both worlds.